The Art of Theatrical Makeup for Stage and Screen

The Art of Theatrical Makeup for Stage and Screen

Michael G. Westmore

Illustrated by Al Mayton

E 70

McGRAW-HILL BOOK COMPANY

New York	Kuala Lumpur	Panama
St. Louis	London	Rio de Janeiro
San Fransisco	Mexico	Singapore
Düsseldorf	Montreal	Sydney
Johannesburg	New Delhi	Toronto

Michael G. Westmore belongs to the third generation of Westmores to create makeup techniques used throughout the world.

After graduation from the University of California at Santa Barbara, as an art history major, Michael Westmore joined the Hollywood Guild of Make-Up Artists (local 706) and the makeup staff at Universal Studio. At Universal he trained under his uncle, Bud Westmore.

During his early professional years, Michael Westmore was fortunate in having worked closely with Academy Award winner John Chambers. From Chambers, Westmore acquired a unique background in laboratory and prosthetic makeup procedures.

A member of the National Academy of Television Arts and Sciences and of other professional organizations, Westmore has worked on numerous motion pictures, stage productions, and television programs.

He has been a consultant on special makeup techniques for the Mark Taper Forum, Los Angeles Music Center, and has designed postoperative makeup styles for people who have undergone cosmetic and corrective facial surgery.

Currently a freelance makeup artist and lecturer, Westmore teaches a class on advanced makeup techniques in the Theater Arts Department at Los Angeles Valley College.

Al Mayton, began his training at the Dallas Museum of Fine Arts. After perfecting his drawing techniques under the guidance of Chapman Kelly, he worked as an animator both in advertising and for the Disney studios. He became art director at the Lorraine Studios in New York City and later served as art director for several trade magazines.

Library of Congress Cataloging in Publication Data
Westmore, Michael G
    The art of theatrical makeup for stage and screen.
    1. Make-up, Theatrical. I. Title.
PN2068.W4 1973   792'.027   72-1795
ISBN 0-07-069485-0

THE ART OF THEATRICAL MAKEUP FOR STAGE AND SCREEN

1234567890EBEB79876543

792.027
W533

The editors for this book were Ardelle Cleverdon and Catherine Kerr, the designer was Marsha Cohen, and its production was supervised by James Lee. It was set in Helvetica by J. C. Meyer. It was printed and bound by Edwards Brothers.

This book is lovingly dedicated to the four deceased members of Hollywood's "Royal Family of Makeup Artists," my grandfather, George Westmore, my father, Monty Westmore, and his brothers, Ern and Perc. Their innovative genius, extensive research, and hard work led to many of today's finest techniques in the art of theatrical makeup.

Contents

Preface

Contemporary actors may use the latest materials and techniques in applying makeup, but they are practicing an art that is thousands of years old. Cosmetics for both the face and body can be traced back to ancient times and to peoples scattered all over the world.

The early use of makeup has been documented by discoveries of wall paintings, stone and pottery artifacts, mummies with painted faces and dyed hair, sculptured pieces, masks, and other relics from past civilizations. The cosmetics were probably used for religious, medical, and decorative reasons.

Over the years, general makeup customs have drastically changed both in style and in acceptance by the public. A few centuries ago, a gentleman was recognized by his powdered wig, yet, only one hundred years later, Victorian women who "painted their faces" were considered wicked.

Customs in theatrical makeup have varied as well. During certain periods of history and in some countries, male actors were made up to resemble women and played female stage roles. Styles in makeup have also undergone extensive modifications. Old motion pictures and television reruns strikingly indicate the various trends within recent years.

Today theatrical makeup is used in motion pictures, on television, and in amateur and professional stage companies. It is utilized for many purposes.

One of the chief reasons is to make the actor look natural in spite of the strong lights used in the theater. Without proper makeup, the face looks washed out, pale, and flat against theater lights. Because few people have perfectly formed faces, makeup can minimize poor features and emphasize good ones. The use of character makeup can produce remarkable results. It gives the actor an extra prop with which to portray his role, and it strengthens the illusionary effect of the character both for performer and audience.

Every actor should be aware of what makeup can do for him. He should realize that amateurish or incorrect makeup techniques can mar his appearance and perhaps spoil his performance. The proper application of theatrical makeup can add a tremendously important embellishment toward a successful production.

This book teaches the latest and most effective procedures in the art of theatrical makeup. Five main areas of the field are covered: Introduction to fundamental aspects of theatrical makeup, basic and corrective makeup, character makeup, techniques with hair, and construction and use of prosthetics.

Each subject is presented in a simple, step-by-step arrangement. The treatment is comprehensive and includes lists of specific materials required, detailed instructions, and complete illustrations. (Periodically, review topics and sample problems have been added to reinforce the material given.)

The procedures are all of professional caliber, yet they can be followed by students ranging from the novice to the expert. The methods will be helpful for student productions at every grade level (elementary through college), for amateur organizations of all kinds, for little theater groups, and for professional companies. Many of the techniques were especially developed through student research in my classes at Los Angeles Valley College.

The use of the theatrical makeup techniques demonstrated in this volume can enhance every production and help each actor achieve a greater sense of satisfaction with his performance.

Michael G. Westmore

The Art of Theatrical Makeup for Stage and Screen

Introduction to Theatrical Makeup

1

The Skull

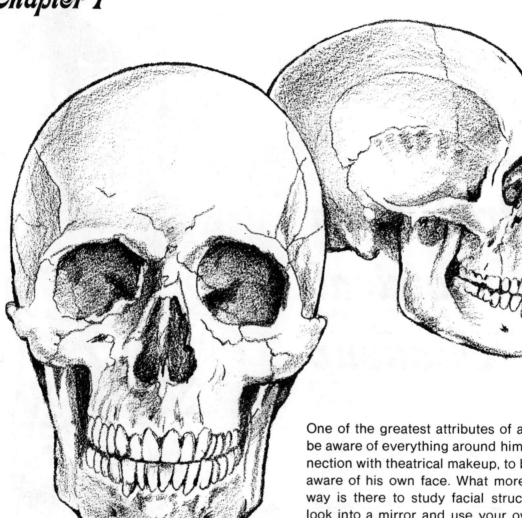

One of the greatest attributes of an artist is to be aware of everything around him and, in connection with theatrical makeup, to be especially aware of his own face. What more convenient way is there to study facial structure than to look into a mirror and use your own image as a guide.

Using either a human skull or illustrations, trace the facial high points and cavities with your fingers. Then discover the same areas on your own face. This will demonstrate the areas where applications of highlight and shadow can be most effective. Highlighting the protruding bones can bring projection into a makeup, and shadowing the cavities can add much depth. The importance of this ability will be seen when the chapters on corrective and character makeups are studied.

Equipment
Preparation

Chapter 2

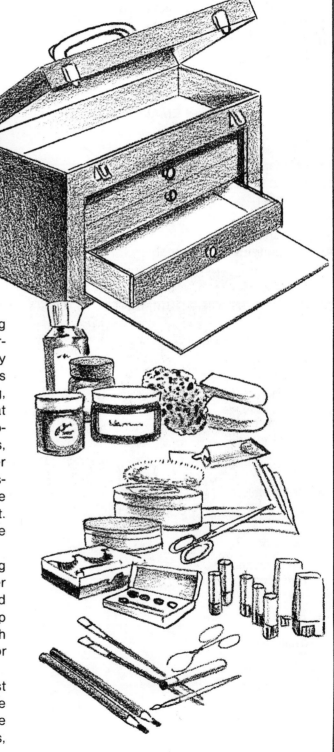

One of the most formidable tasks in beginning your study of makeup is the collecting and purchasing of supplies. Due to the great popularity of cosmetics today many of the basic materials can be directly purchased at local variety, drug, specialty, and department stores, as well as at craft and paint centers. Large theatrical suppliers, located on the East and West coasts, carry items not readily available. This chapter is designed to be used as a checklist. All necessary materials are listed by category for the collection of a complete theatrical makeup kit. As additional items are added, they should be noted for future reference.

It is equally important to see what is being done as it is to apply and wear makeup. If proper lighting conditions are not available, one should purchase a travel or portable type of makeup mirror with lights. If possible, the room in which makeup is applied should be neutral in color to prevent any inaccurate light reflections.

First, a makeup case or carrying kit must be acquired. It should be partitioned off inside and be large enough to accommodate all the materials needed to create various makeups, hairpieces, and prosthetics.

BASIC EQUIPMENT—MALE

1. Makeup case
2. Base makeup
3. White rubber sponge
4. Dark brown eyebrow pencil
5. Powder puff or cotton
6. Translucent or tinted powder
7. Artist's water color brush no. 8 flat
8. Cleansing cream
9. Tissues
10. Hand mirror

BASIC EQUIPMENT—FEMALE

All of the above plus:
11. Mascara
12. Rouge
13. Eyeliner
14. Lipstick
15. Eye shadow
Additional items are optional.

DETAILED LIST OF EQUIPMENT

1. Base Makeup Colors

   Straight base
   Highlight
   Shadow
   Under base
   Dark shade
   Clown white
   Black
   Assorted

2. Body Makeup

   To match base makeup

3. Sponge

   White rubber
   Red stipple
   Yellow sea or animal

4. Powder

   Translucent
   Tinted
   Talc
   Powder puff

5. Brushes

   Powder
   Spirit gum (½-inch casine)

   Eyebrow brush or toothbrush
   Assorted water color brushes (flats nos. 1 to 12, 16, 18, 20; rounds no. 00 short, or long nos. 1 to 10, 12, 14, 16, 18, 20)

6. Pencils

   Black
   Dark brown
   Medium brown
   Light brown
   Auburn
   Red
   Green
   Blue
   Maroon
   Gray drafting pencil

7. Eye Shadow (dry and/or moist)

   Brown
   Gray
   Blue
   Green
   White or pale
   Assorted

8. Mascara (cake or roller)

   Black
   Brown

9. Eyeliner (cake or liquid)

   Black
   Brown

10. Rouge (dry brush-on, moist, or liquid)

    Pink
    Peach
    Coral
    Tawny

11. Lipstick

    Pink
    Coral
    Orange
    Red
    Natural
    Lip gloss

12. Miscellaneous

    Cover makeup
    Eyelashes
    Eyelash adhesive
    Astringent
    Skin freshener
    Moisturizer
    Cotton
    Cotton swabs
    Razor blades
    Tissue
    Hair cloth

Castor oil
Facial spray (makeup set)

ADDITIONAL SUPPLIES FOR CHARACTER MAKEUP

1. Rubber grease base
2. Blood
3. Modeling wax
4. Plastic sealer or surgical spray bandage
5. Liners or grease colors in shades of brown, blue, green, yellow, gray, red, purple, maroon, black, and white
6. Plastic bottles that will fit into kit (to hold liquids)

HAIR SUPPLIES

1. Adhesives

   Spirit gum
   Liquid latex

2. Crepe Wool

   Light blond
   Dark blond
   Light brown
   Medium brown
   Dark brown
   Auburn
   White
   Gray
   Black

3. Sprays

   Hair spray
   Color sprays
   Clear acrylic spray

4. Moustache Wax

   White
   Brown

5. Combs

   Barber
   Tail

6. Scissors

   Hair-cutting
   Utility

7. Hair Dressing

   Conditioner—lanolin
   Setting-nonoily

8. Tweezers

CLEAN-UP

1. Soap
2. Towels
3. Cold cream
4. Shampoo
5. Acetone
6. Clens makeup remover
7. Alcohol
8. Wig cleaner

The following describes the specific preparation of some materials needed in the makeup kit:

SPONGES

White Rubber Sponge A finely pored white rubber sponge. This can be purchased from cosmetic beauty suppliers or upholstery shops. For best control and application the sponge should be cut into an oblong shape approximately 1 by 1 by 3 inches and tapered at one end.

Stipple Sponge A coarsely pored red or gray sponge. A good substitute is the soft sponge used in filtering systems of heaters and air conditioners; it should also be cut into oblong shapes approximately 1 by 1 by 2 inches and ½ by ½ by 2 inches. A variety of sizes will add versatility to your efforts. The end of the stipple sponge should be rounded with a pair of scissors; the sponge will then create circular patterns of color when applied.

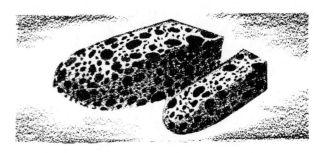

Sea or Natural Sponge A natural sea sponge sold in beauty and variety stores. The small ones are used for the face and the larger ones for the body.

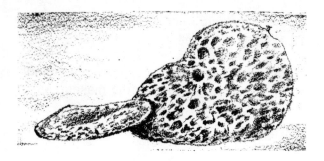

WOOD EYEBROW PENCILS— THEATRICALLY SHARPENED

A wood eyebrow pencil can best be used if it is cut into a theatrical style or chisel shape. The pencil should be cooled before cutting because warm lead has a tendency to bend or break.

1. Hold the pencil in one hand, approximately 2 inches from the end to be cut.

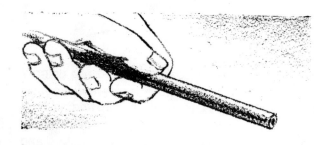

2. With a single-edge utility razor blade, begin to shave off the end until the midway area is reached.

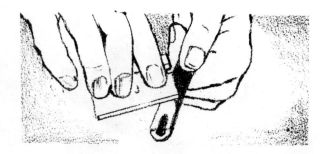

3. Turn the pencil over and shave the other side to match. Make several small strokes to complete the trimming; a single cut might break the lead.

4. Turn the pencil from side to side and shave off the remaining wood.
   This will produce a multipurpose eyebrow pencil. By using it on the narrow side, fine hairline strokes can be created. The wide side can be used for broad strokes of coloring or blending. Every pencil in a makeup kit should be cut in this style and kept sharp.

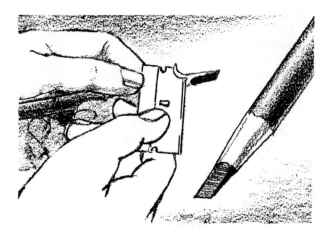

LIQUID LATEX

The following are three types of liquid latex; each one has a specific purpose.

Latex (Liquid) Adhesive This is a thin latex which can be used for applying prosthetics, stippling on the face for old age and character, or covering prosthetic edges. Latex adhesive is an all-purpose makeup latex.

Foam (Liquid) Latex Due to its structure this latex is best suited to be mixed with other chemicals to form foam latex. (See Chapter 37.)

Slip-casting Latex This is a heavy liquid latex which is used for bald caps, cap wig bases, and hollow prosthetics and masks. It can be painted on the surface of a plaster mold to form a tough latex skin, or it can be poured into a negative mold to set for a specific time so as to build up on the plaster surface through absorption.

With use and time any liquid latex will become thick and creamy due to water evaporation. To restore the latex, add a small amount of distilled water. Combine a tablespoon of water at a time, thoroughly mixing each spoonful as it is added, until the original consistency has been restored.

Starting a
Picture File

Chapter 3

Before developing any historical, racial, or character type of makeup, it is necessary to study related pictures and other reference materials. Every actor should continually collect and file facial pictures from all periods of history, as well as pictures of nationalities and unique types of modern faces suitable for development into interesting characters.

Magazines, both domestic and foreign, are excellent sources for national and character faces. Art history books are also good sources for period styles. You can often find pictures in advertising circulars, souvenir publications, theatrical handbills and programs, posters, etc. Every conscientious artist collects pictures so that he or she may always be ready to do something unusual, and moreover to do it accurately and with self-confidence.

Makeup Charts

Chapter 4

Pictures and charts are among the most worthwhile records of past makeups. Pictures are useful because they show the completed makeup; however, a chart based on a simple line drawing of a face can include a detailed list of every cosmetic and product used, as well as the exact areas of application.

The makeup chart included in this text should be used as an example. It should be duplicated and used by the artist as a record of all successful makeups. Carefully file these charts in a morgue and you will never have to ask yourself, "How did I do that?"

Production _____ No. _____

Character _____ Date _____

Performer _____ Makeup Artist _____

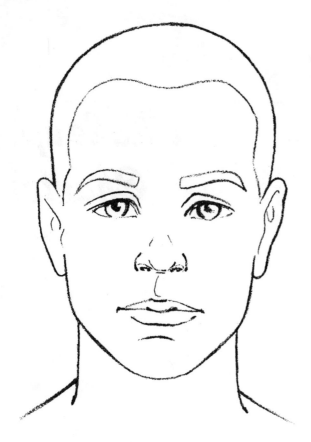 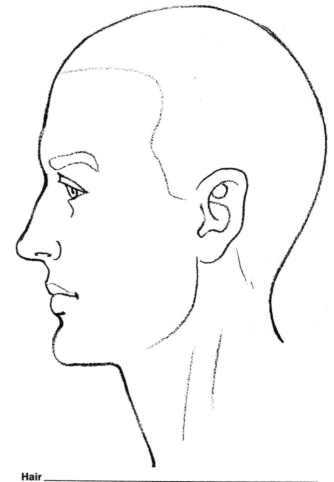

MALE MAKEUP CHART

COLORING

Foundation _____

Highlights _____

Shadow _____

Eye Shadow _____

Lip Rouge _____

Makeup Pencil _____

Mascara _____

Under Rouge _____

Dry Rouge _____

Body Makeup _____

Hair _____

NOTES _____

_____

_____

_____

_____

_____

_____

_____

_____

Production _____ **No.** _____

Character _____ **Date** _____

Performer _____ **Makeup Artist** _____

FEMALE MAKEUP CHART

COLORING

Foundation _____

Highlights _____

Shadow _____

Eye Shadow _____

Lip Rouge _____

Makeup Pencil _____

Mascara _____

Under Rouge _____

Dry Rouge _____

Body Makeup _____

Hair _____

NOTES _____

_____

_____

_____

_____

_____

_____

_____

_____

The Student may reproduce this page only, for his or her private use without further written permission from the publisher.

Mass reproduction for sale or free distribution is prohibited under the copyright of this book.

Makeup Charts

11

Chapter 5

Before a complicated makeup is created, a prototype is developed to work out any problems. This prototype is called a visual overlay; it saves the makeup artist time and expense when developing a new character. After the desired makeup has been styled on a clear sheet of acetate, placed over a photograph, the artist will have a precise understanding of what is needed for the finished product.

Materials:

8- by 10-inch black and white photograph of the subject's face

8- by 10-inch sheet of clear or matt acetate

Acrylic paint in assorted colors or Prismacolor pencils

Clear tape

Assorted artist's brushes

Research material

Method:

1. Tape the acetate to the top of the photograph, leaving the bottom and the sides free.

2. With the brushes, acrylic paint, and the research materials, create the desired character by painting on the acetate which is over the photograph. If you prefer to work with dry media, use Prismacolor pencils on matt-finish acetate. Place the acetate, matt side up, over the photograph. Secure it on the top and sketch the makeup design.

3. Insert a piece of white paper between the acetate and the photograph; this will provide a guide for the amount of work and makeup needed to develop the character.

Lighting and Wardrobe Coordination

Chapter 6

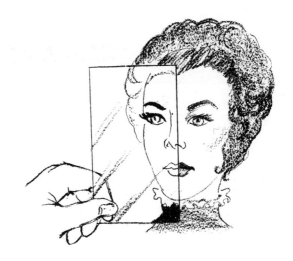

Lighting can be an aid or a detriment. Light can cause makeup to fade, darken, turn white, or change colors; if the proper makeup effect is not initially achieved, corrections can be made with the lights, and errors in makeup can be corrected by the toning down, darkening, or changing of the base shade and lining colors.

A simple way to see the principal effects of lighting is to look at applied makeup shades and colors through the gels to be used; this process is especially necessary if there is to be a predominance of one color. As an example, red lights will wash out any red in makeup, but green lights will turn red colors black, especially red lipstick. Therefore, with the use of different kinds of lightings, strange effects can be turned to an advantage.

Improper wardrobe and staging can be just as detrimental to a performance as poor makeup. Decoration and clothing styles from various periods can easily be found in reference books, especially in the art history section of the library.

Budgeting

Chapter 7

Due to the cost of making up a large number of actors for many performances, it is worthwhile to arrange a common makeup budget. A responsible person should be chosen to total all the supplies needed by the individual performers and then contact the various sources for the best possible discounts and prices. Substantial savings can usually be made through quantity purchasing. Because of continually rising costs, it has recently become the responsibility of the performer to purchase the materials he or she will need. More money can then be allotted to other areas of the production.

Because of hygiene considerations, esthetics, and an actor's personal needs, each performer must have his or her own kit. It is most unprofessional to borrow another performer's tools.

Terminology of Application

Chapter 8

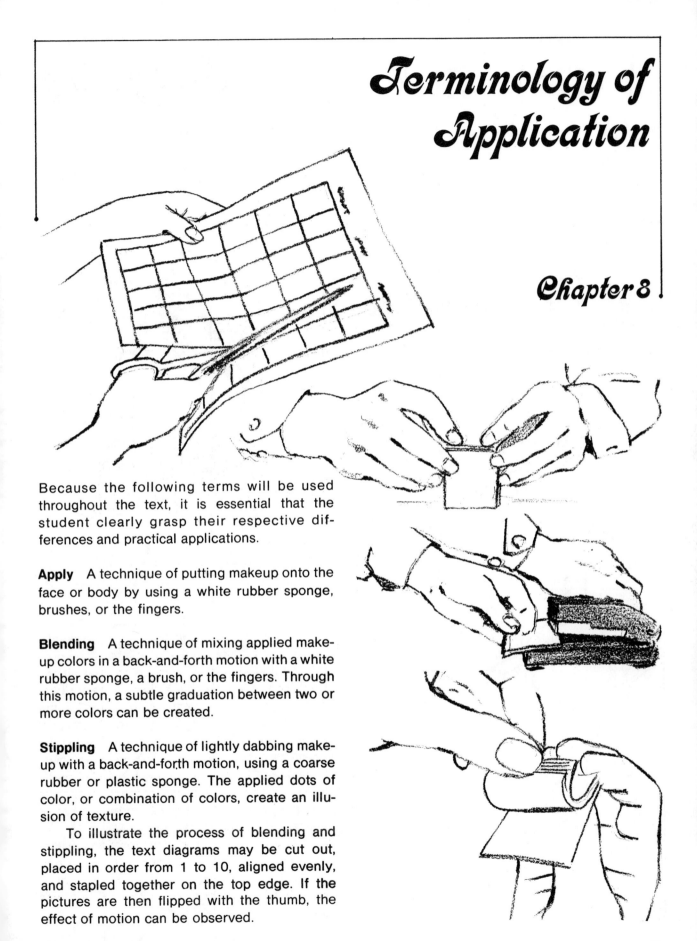

Because the following terms will be used throughout the text, it is essential that the student clearly grasp their respective differences and practical applications.

Apply   A technique of putting makeup onto the face or body by using a white rubber sponge, brushes, or the fingers.

Blending   A technique of mixing applied makeup colors in a back-and-forth motion with a white rubber sponge, a brush, or the fingers. Through this motion, a subtle graduation between two or more colors can be created.

Stippling   A technique of lightly dabbing makeup with a back-and-forth motion, using a coarse rubber or plastic sponge. The applied dots of color, or combination of colors, create an illusion of texture.

To illustrate the process of blending and stippling, the text diagrams may be cut out, placed in order from 1 to 10, aligned evenly, and stapled together on the top edge. If the pictures are then flipped with the thumb, the effect of motion can be observed.

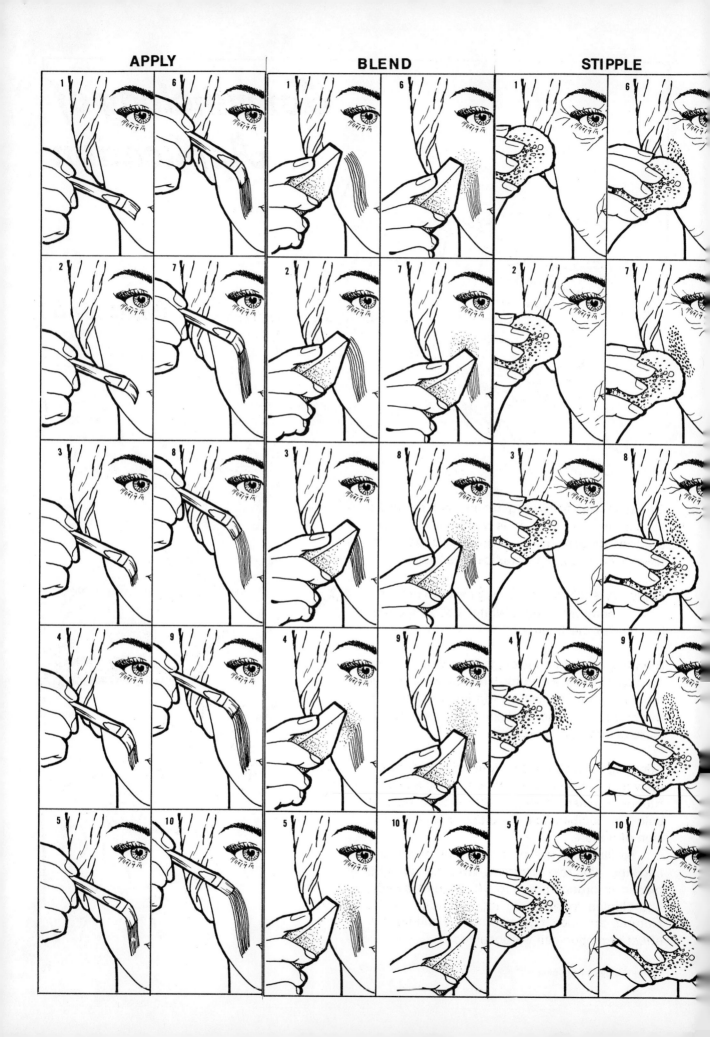

SECTION ONE REVIEW

This text is designed to build knowledge and skill in a special sequence, so the material previously discussed must be understood before the student continues. The following review covers Chapters 1 to 9. The exercises can be done on either an individual or group basis.

1. What is the purpose of wearing theatrical makeup?
2. To show your understanding of the areas of highlight and shadow, shade in on a chart the areas of depth, and indicate the areas of protrusion.
3. List three types of sponge used in the application of makeup.
4. Explain the purpose of a theatrically sharpened pencil.
5. What is the importance of maintaining a picture file? Begin your file by collecting a picture of an American Indian, a clown, an Oriental, an old man or woman.
6. What is the purpose of charting a completed makeup?
7. Construct and paint a "visual overlay."
8. Collect several colors of construction paper (red, green, blue, yellow, etc.) and mount them on a board. Look at the paper through individually colored gels and note the results.
9. List names, addresses, and phone numbers of local stores where supplies can be purchased.
10. Define and demonstrate the techniques of applying, blending, and stippling.

Basic and Corrective Makeup

Al Mayton

19

Skin Care

COLD CREAM

Before the application of basic makeup techniques is explained, it's important to analyze the condition and care of the skin. If a performer has perfectly toned skin, makeup will spread and adhere to it easily; but if the skin is dry or oily, it will appear blotchy or smeared due to variations in absorption. The correction for dry skin is the daily use of a moisturizer applied before base makeup and after the face is cleaned following a performance.

If the problem is an oily complexion, a quick and thorough wipe with a facial toner or astringent will remove excess oil and allow the makeup to spread smoothly.

Just as important as prior skin conditioning is proper makeup removal after a performance. Poor cleansing habits lead to skin problems. I hereby recommend any commercial facial cleanser that can be followed by a washing with warm water and soap and a closing of the pores with cool water. This simple cleansing method will also give an exhausted performer a little lift after the final curtain.

Performers with skin allergies or other unusual conditions should consult with a doctor before applying any cosmetics, commercial cleansers, etc., to the face.

The following list suggests what to use for cleaning both the skin and the tools.

1. Cold cream or Clens makeup remover—for removal of grease makeup.
2. Soap and water—for removal of water-soluble makeup.
3. Clens makeup remover or isopropyl alcohol —for removal of spirit gum from the face.
4. Acetone—for removal of spirit gum from tools and hair goods (avoid contact with the skin and plastic tools).
5. Wig cleaner—to clean wigs, hairpieces, and makeup brushes. Brushes must be frequently cleaned for reasons of hygiene and to ensure the purity of applied colors.

Base Makeup
Selection

Chapter 10

In current theatrical productions, the tendency is for performers to appear natural and less heavily made up than in previous years. For a straight makeup, the performer should present a natural, clean, healthy glow when viewed from all angles of the theatre.

Makeup supply charts can be acquired from the major theatrical distributors. Upon request, they will furnish a list of the various shades with the recommended uses. I suggest you write some of these sources for this information to refer to later for research and purchases.

Because of individual skin tones, it is impossible to recommend a specific base shade for everyone. In many cases it is not always necessary to purchase theatrical names and numbers of makeup. The base shades and cosmetic accessories available to the general public in department, variety, and drug stores will suffice nicely. Assistance is usually available from the cosmetic sales representative in the stores where locally distributed cosmetics are sold. Select bases that have been formulated with opacity, so that highlight and shadow will blend smoothly.

Skin coloring has four basic tones: brown, fair, pink, and olive. In selecting base colors for skin tones of fair, pink, and olive, choose shades of olive, beige, or suntan. These should be in a shade compatible with the natural skin tone, but one to several shades deeper.

The depth of tone depends on the character, size of the theater, and the intensity of the lighting. On smaller stages, with subtle lighting, lighter shades of base makeup are most appropriate. You will need to make your own selection; few actors make up the same or wear the same color base. Persons with predominantly pink or ruddy complexions must avoid any base containing red and select instead a base color with cool undertones.

Persons with brown skin tones should select matching base shades or a base one shade deeper than the natural skin tone. With the ever-expanding market in cosmetics for brown skin tones, no one should have difficulty selecting a base color from local department stores.

In future discussions, people with pink, fair, and olive skin tones will be grouped together in the category referred to as people with fair complexions. People with skin tones in varying shades of brown will be referred to as having brown complexions.

Basic and Corrective Makeup

Basic Makeup Application

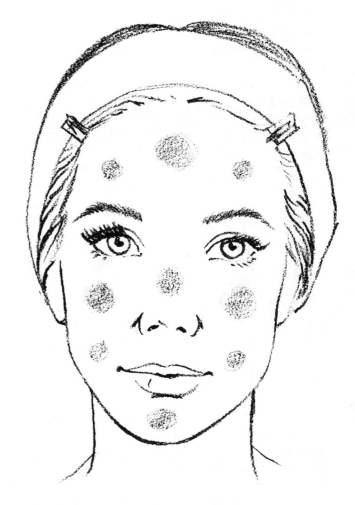

Chapter 11

This chapter contains the basic techniques for the application of straight theatrical makeup for men and women with either fair or brown complexions. The principles apply to both sexes, but men should be subtle in applying makeup.

MATERIALS

Base makeup

Moist and/or dry rouge

Moist and/or dry eye shadow

Yellow animal sponge

Eyeliner·

Eyebrow pencil

Translucent or tinted powder

Powder puff

White rubber sponge

Mascara

False lashes

Lipstick

Assorted brushes

Tissue

APPLICATION

Base Makeup   After the appropriate shade is chosen, it is ready to be applied with a piece of white rubber sponge or the fingers. Many professional performers prefer to apply makeup with the fingers because the warmth from the hands tends to soften the makeup. The fingers are used like multiple sponges smoothing and spreading on the color.

Dot the makeup around the face with sponge or fingers. Spread it on so that the face is completely covered with a thin coat of base. Heavy applications make the face look aged and crepey. Chapter 9 on skin care has been written in conjunction with base makeup application and should be consulted regarding dry and oily skin conditions. For additional preconditioning of slightly dry skin, add a little baby oil to the sponge or face before applying the base. For extremely dry or sunburned skin, stipple a thin coat of castor oil over the face before applying the base shade. The castor oil is not readily absorbed and offers makeup a foundation on which to adhere.

Cover the neck, ears, and into the hairline with base; otherwise, areas not made up will appear extremely white under the lights.

Rouge The purpose of using moist and dry rouge is to add color to the face and to break up the flatness that would occur if the base were used alone.

Fair complexions are enhanced by soft shades of pink and peach, while brown complexions are best accented with coral and tawny shades. The choice of color, therefore, is very critical.

Moist rouge is applied before powder, whereas dry or brush-on rouge is used to accent the already powdered makeup.

For correct placement, rough is applied on the cheek bone area and then gently blended

into the hairline and base. Avoid applying rouge too low on the cheeks or next to the nose because this tends to create a character effect rather than a natural one.

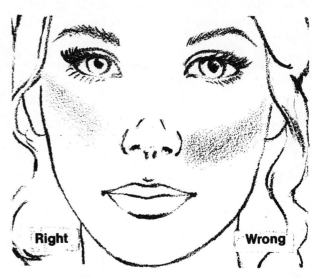

Right   Wrong

How much rouge is needed? A simple test in front of the lights will tell. Remember, subtlety is the key to naturalness.

Eye Shadow (Grease and Dry) Grease or stick shadow is applied to the eyelid area and blended out toward the eyebrow before powder is added; dry shadows can be used alone or to intensify and touch up the color underneath.

Care must be exercised when you choose a color. Dark shades deepen the eye sockets, creating a skull-like effect, and unnatural colors will appear phony and amateurish.

Everyone should use discretion when wearing green or blue shadow on the stage. These colors should be reserved for character roles.

To create a natural stage makeup, browns and grays are best for fair complexions. People with brown complexions should use lighter shadows such as toast, mushroom, or soft yellows to help enhance the eyes.

The amount of makeup needed to project facial contours will depend again upon the size and lighting of the theater.

Powdering When powdering, apply a generous amount. The most powder that can be packed into the base will give the most lasting makeup. Under-powdering will cause the skin oils to break through very quickly, producing an un-

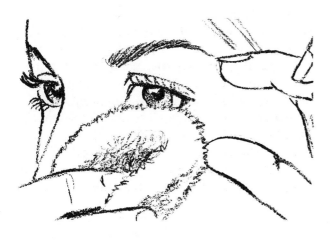

wanted shine. If necessary, using the thumb and forefinger, draw the skin tightly so as to work powder into any lines and creases. After applying powder to the entire face, starting under and around the eyes, continue to press it in gently

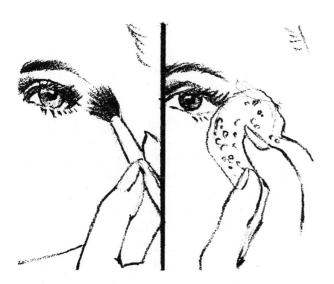

for a full thirty seconds. Brush off the excess powder wth a large soft brush or a piece of cotton; then wet a natural sponge or cotton and lightly wipe across the face. This technique will

set the makeup, erase any visible powder, and take away the masky feeling.

Translucent powders have proved most successful for fair complexions, as they do not change the original color of the base, the under-rouge, or the moist eye shadow. Brown complexions should be set with tinted powder that is compatible with the base color. Use it sparingly over the under-rouge and moist eye shadow. As noted before, dry rouge and dry eye shadow should be applied after the entire face is powdered.

Lining the Eyes Liquid eyeliner, cake eyeliner, or the theatrically cut wood eyebrow pencil (black or dark brown) is used to accent and frame the eyes. Care must be exercised when eyes are made up, because they are the most expressive feature of the face. They are one of the actor's main areas of communication.

Upper Line
Using the eyeliner brush or the sharp end of the eyebrow pencil, start at the inside corner of the eye and thinly draw it all the way along

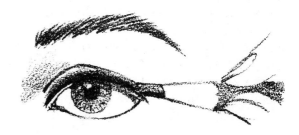

the eyelid close to the lashes. There are two styles with which to finish the lining of the upper lid. One style is the extended line, which gives length and creates the almond-shaped eye. The other style is the nonextended line with the heaviness over the center. The second style is used for widening, and it has been called the owl eye. Experiment with both styles until you discover which is more attractive for you. If the

sharpness of a straight line is not desired, use the wide cut of the wood pencil. Start at the inside corner of the eye, draw it along the eyelid next to the liner. Softly blend the liner and the pencil color up over the eyelid so that they fade into the shadow color of the eyelid area. For the male a more subtle effect is preferable, and blended pencil across the lids is usually sufficient.

Lower Line

Under the eye, using the same liner or pencil, apply a thin line. Do not begin this line at the inside corner because, due to framing, it will make the eye appear smaller. Using the thinner

portion of the pencil or brush, begin the line ¼ inch from the inside corner and draw the line under and next to the lower lashes. At the end of the line, extend the line slightly to create the illusion of a wider eye. The line should be smudged for softness with the fingers or a cotton stick directly under the eye. Another technique for lining under the eye is drawing

individual lashes. These are sketched directly under the eye and should be angled in the direction of natural growth. This method, correctly applied, is extremely effective.

Shaping and Coloring the Eyebrows The shaping of the eyebrow is exceedingly important because, in their very shape and contour, eyebrows dramatically express emotions. A raised brow denotes surprise, while a drooping brow expresses sadness. From these examples, it's

easy to understand why a natural brow style is most effective in a straight makeup.

I recommend that people of all complexions, when in doubt as to which color to use, start with a soft gray pencil. To begin, lightly use it to mark out the basic shape. Then go over this with fine hairline strokes, using a color that matches the natural hair color. If the natural hair coloring is very light, the gray pencil will suffice.

When using the pencil to shape the brows, it is best to cut it in the theatrical manner. This type of sharpening will enable the artist to make fine hairline strokes. The following is a general pattern which may be used as a guide for making up a natural brow.

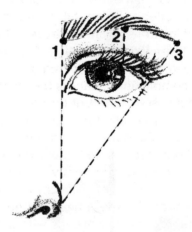

1. Always brush and draw the eyebrows in the direction of the natural growth of hair.
2. Begin the eyebrow by drawing an imaginary line along the outside of the nose and the inside of the eye. This is point 1. It should also be the widest part of the brow.
3. Look straight ahead and draw an imaginary line up from the outside edge of the iris. This is where the arch will be. Be sure to taper the brow all the way from point 1 to point 2.
4. Draw another imaginary line from the corner of the nose beyond the outside corner of the eye. At an angle of 45°, down from point 2, is point 3. This is where the brow

Basic and Corrective Makeup

should end in a very fine, soft taper.

For men the simplest care of a brow is darkening it with the broad side of the pencil and filling in any sparse areas with fine hairline strokes. To carefully color each hair, first moisten an eyebrow pencil with a drop of baby oil and rub it across an old toothbrush; then use the brush to lightly brush through the eyebrow hairs.

Shaping and coloring the eyebrows is crucial and requires much time and practice.

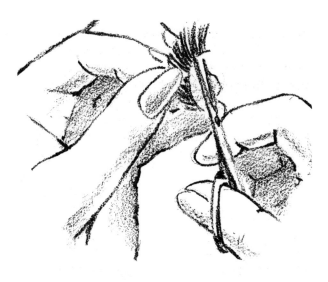

2. If a lash base is too long for the eye, trim it off from the outside, removing a few hairs at a time.

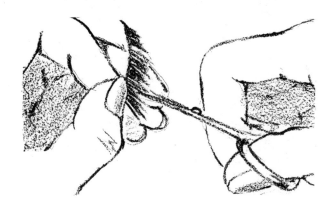

Mascara For an added device to accent the eyes, brush mascara across the lashes. Simply moisten the roller or brush, fill it with mascara, and apply it in strokes from the base of the lash in the direction away from the eye. For the stage the lower lashes should be coated also. For fair and brown complexions, black is the most popular and widely used color, but for very fair complexions, and especially for men, dark brown is sufficient. A procedure to add body to the lashes, without resorting to the wearing of false lashes, is to mascara and lightly powder them; then successive coats of mascara are applied until the desired thickness has built up on the lashes. The process always ends with a coat of mascara.

3. If the false lash hairs are too long, trim them with cuticle scissors, cutting the hairs so that some of them will be left longer than others. If you do this, the lash will retain its natural feathery appearance.
4. False lashes should be handled carefully. They will last much longer if the specific directions for commercial lash cleaners are followed.

False Eyelashes In place of powder and mascara, false lashes may be worn. Either of these techniques will define the eyes. I will not discuss the application of false lashes here, because most manufacturers include instructions with their products. However, the following general hints may be helpful.

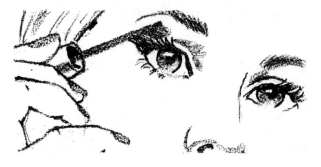

1. Surgical adhesive is the best adhering agent and is easily removed when lashes are cleaned.

5. After applying false lashes, be sure to mascara the natural ones into them.

6. Caution should be taken when a pair of lashes are purchased for the stage, even if the audience doesn't see them at close range. An attractive style should be chosen within a medium range of thickness. For people with brown complexions a heavier lash is more becoming than a thinner one.

7. To present a natural appearance, the false lash hairs may be individually applied to both top and bottom lashes. You can obtain these hairs by cutting up an old pair of lashes. Dot the ends with adhesive and place them among the natural ones. This procedure takes much time and practice; it can never be left until just before the performance.

Lipstick The eye area is second only to the lips in importance. The eyes and ears of the audience follow mouth movements as an important channel of communication. Underplayed or overplayed lips detract from a performer and a performance.

The larger the mouth, the deeper the lipstick tone should be, but it should not be deep enough to make the actor appear "all mouth." Too dark a lipstick will draw the eye directly to the mouth; conversely, too light a lipstick causes the lips to vanish. Lighting is an important additional consideration, because lipstick changes color under extreme lighting conditions.

Fair complexions are best complimented by the medium range of lipsticks in natural shades —pink and coral. Brown complexions are best enhanced by natural shades of coral and orange. The use of red shades should be reserved for very large theaters and character portrayals.

After applying the lipstick, line the lips with an auburn or brown pencil for a natural yet well-defined mouth.

Lipstick on men must be applied with caution or it will make a man appear doll-like. If lipstick is used by men, it should be in a natural shade lightly applied.

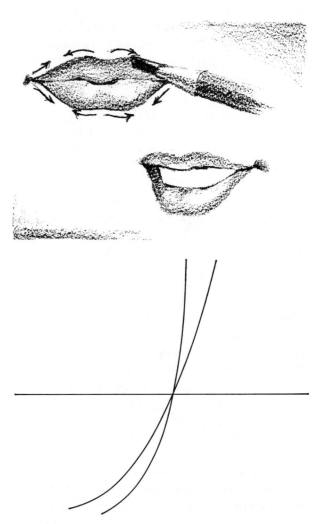

Basic and Corrective Makeup

Corrective Makeup

Chapter 12

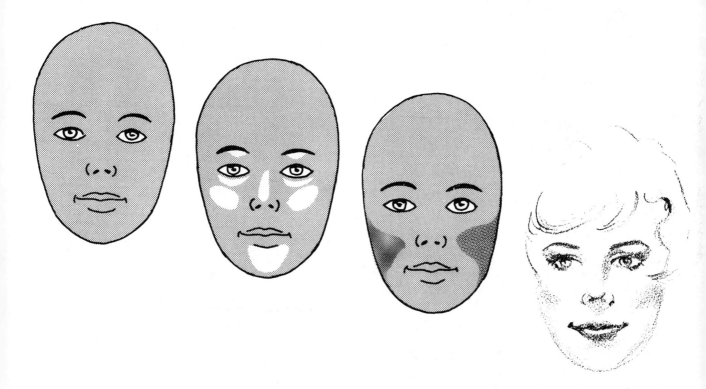

After you are adept at doing a straight makeup, you are ready for the next step, corrective makeup. Though commonly referred to as corrective makeup, this process is actually the art of highlight and shadow. With highlight and shadow, illusions can be created on the face where none actually exist. A face is altered with this technique; areas can be made to stand out or to recede. Both of these results are achieved by the use of different-colored base makeups, liner colors, and/or dry shadows. To bring out

an area of the face, a highlight is applied over the base. A highlight is a base makeup that is at least two shades lighter than the base or one made by the mixture of a small amount of base and some white grease. The customary areas to be brought out are the bridge of the nose, cheekbones, and places under the eyes and below the brows. Blend out the highlight thoroughly before applying any shadows. When blended simultaneously, the two colors combine into a muddy shade.

The methods described should be used according to the artist's discretion. As a guideline, he should simply remember that lighter colors increase the light reflection and prominence of an area. Darker colors absorb more light and tend to minimize the area.

Conversely, an illusion of depth and definition is created when a color at least two shades darker than the base makeup is applied over the base shade. Preferably, shadows for corrective makeup should be done in a warm brown, with a cast of red or orange. The usual areas to be deepened are the eye sockets, the sides of the

nose (for thinning), cheeks (for shallowing), and flesh under the chin (to minimize heaviness). Highlights or shadows should be applied to an area slightly smaller than the final size of the desired effect; this restriction is necessary to compensate for the spreading that results from blending.

MAJOR FAULTS OF STAGE MAKEUP

Lip Correction If the lips appear too thin, it's advisable to paint them in by going over the natural lip line. The word "paint" is used be-

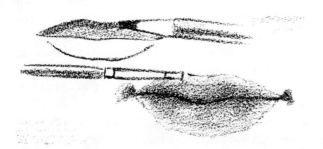

cause the best results are achieved with a lip brush. You can increase the illusion of a fuller lip line by lining the outside of the lip with a red, auburn, or brown pencil. For lips that are too prominent, a lighter shade of lipstick can be used on the outside to minimize the shape.

For lips that change color and lips that smear, apply a coat of lipstick, then powder, blot with damp cotton, and apply a second coat of lipstick. To tone down naturally dark lips, apply a thin coat of base makeup over them.

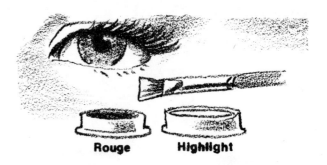

Rouge   Highlight

Discoloration under the Eyes On many people a bluish discoloration is found around or under the eyes. A little extra sleep often remedies this condition. If not, some highlight can be put directly on the discoloration after the makeup base is applied. If there is extreme discoloration, mix a small amount of rouge into the highlight; the pink or coral tones in the rouge will diminish or remove the bluish tones of the skin. This should be applied and powdered before the base color is put on.

Blemishes and Ruddy (Red) Complexions For a complexion with a red area that should be toned down, mix a small amount of green or yellow grease makeup into a light shade of base makeup. Apply this sparingly where needed, cover with powder, and then stipple the regular base makeup over it.

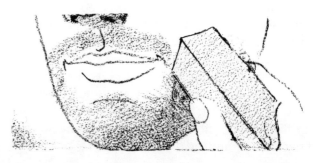

Basic and Corrective Makeup

Covering Heavy Beard Lines Occasionally there is a man whose beard is so heavy that he usually looks unshaven. The same methods used to cover discoloration apply here. Mix a small amount of rouge into a light base color, apply it to the beard shadow, powder, and stipple normal base color over it. This is known as an "under base."

Another quick technique is to cover it with a pressed powdered makeup that has a slightly warm tone.

Under bases that contain yellow, instead of white, are best used to cover discoloration and beard shadows in people with brown complexions.

With regard to the problems mentioned in Chapter 13, the theatrical solutions offered can ordinarily be devised from the standard makeup kit. Commercial cosmetic companies have also recognized a great need for corrective products; therefore, many specialized products can now be purchased from local cosmetic sources.

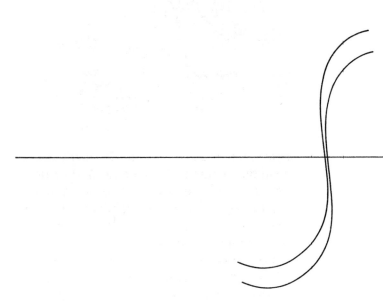

Body Makeup

Chapter 13

Body makeup plays an essential role in completing a performer's makeup because it coordinates the entire character. Every time a pale hand is placed alongside a madeup face, the illusion is broken and the audience is made sharply conscious of makeup. Following are several kinds of cosmetics which can be used to cover the body.

Theatrical (Dry, Water-soluble) Cake Makeup
This should be applied with a special solution made of three parts water to one part astringent or freshener. Wet a natural sponge with the solution, squeeze out the excess, wipe it across the makeup, and apply it to the body. The sponge should not be too dry or too wet; these problems can be remedied by a little practice.

After applying the makeup, smooth it out until there are no streaks, use the hands to do this before all the liquid has evaporated. After it has dried, the makeup can be rubbed down with a soft cloth or powder puff to remove any excess that could spot the wardrobe. Powder any makeup around the neck, wrists, and bustline with corn starch to protect the wardrobe.

Leg Makeup (Opaque), Body Tints, and Gels
These are manufactured by commercial cosmetic companies and may be purchased at local cosmetic counters. These products may be used on the entire body. Before purchasing, be sure to read carefully the directions for application and removal.

BODY MAKEUP CORRECTIONS

Highlight and shadow can be applied to the body as well as the face. The same principles that apply to the face also apply here.

The most important correction is the covering of scars and tattoos. You must first neutralize any scar or tattoo before making it invisible. If the problem area is too light, it must be covered with a grease makeup that will match the natural skin tone. If the area is dark, such as a tattoo or birthmark, it must be covered with a light shade of grease markup. Tattoos should be handled by the same procedure used to cover heavy beard shadows. After applying the under-base makeup, powder it well, and cover over it with an opaque body makeup. Remember to stipple the body color over the treated area so as not to remove the under base. If body makeup

appears flat after being applied, rub a small amount of Vaseline petroleum jelly or cocoa butter on the palms of the hands and pat lightly over the makeup.

Slick Scar   Spirit Gum   Powder   Base Makeup

COVERING OLD SCARS

Many healed scars leave a light slick surface to which makeup will not adhere. Paint just the scar with spirit gum, dry it, powder, and stipple the base makeup over it. The gum will create a foundation to which the base can adhere. Large scars and blemishes are covered by stippling a corrective rubber grease base on the area, powdering, and then adding an opaque body makeup.

Never apply makeup over an open scar, open blemish, or skin rash without first consulting a doctor.

Natural Hair Care

Chapter 14

All performers should know that proper care and grooming of natural hair is a necessary health habit. The following basic suggestions apply equally to men and women, and to persons of all skin tones, because the information pertains only to the hair and scalp. In each statement there are references to specialized products or additional treatments for the hair and scalp, formulated for the specific problems. In caring for natural hair you should use only hard rubber combs and natural-bristle brushes. Other types of grooming aids tend to damage hair and split ends.

Shampooing Performing demands that the hair and the scalp be cleaned frequently. Depending upon the individual hair condition (normal, dry, or oily), a corresponding shampoo should be selected and used regularly. For bleached or tinted hair, a mild nondetergent shampoo such as baby shampoo should be chosen.

34

Oily Hair Natural oiliness comes from the scalp, not from the hair itself. After using a shampoo for oily hair, rinse the hair and scalp thoroughly with cool water to close the pores. The hair should be set with a specialized product for oily hair and be allowed to dry naturally or in a hair dryer set at cool to medium heat. A spray containing extra alcohol should be used on the hair after it has been combed out.

Dry Hair Again there are specialized products for shampooing, setting, and conditioning; these should contain as little alcohol as possible, because alcohol is drying. Dry hair should also be dried naturally or in a dryer set at cool to medium.

Dull Hair This condition should be treated like dry hair. To add extra shine to dull hair, light oil or grease dressing can be used sparingly.

Hard-to-manage Hair Greaseless hair creams and sprays should be used to bring the condition under control.

Gray Hair Special products have also been developed to keep the gray color from yellowing. A special water-type rinse can be applied to brighten gray hair.

Hair Conditioners To be revitalized, natural hair should be conditioned, after shampooing, at least every two weeks. The condition of some hair may warrant more frequent treatments. A protein conditioner is best suited for normal and oily hair, whereas cholesterol or oil conditioners are designed for dry hair.

Snarls Snarls should be worked out of the hair when it is wet. If the hair is dry, a light mist of oil spray will act as a lubricant. Start at the ends of the hair and slowly comb or brush out all snarls. A hard rubber comb or natural-bristle brush is the best tool for this job.

Kinky Hair Specialized products have been developed to straighten kinky hair, but they dry out the hair excessively. A mild conditioner should be applied following the straightening procedure.

Dandruff This can be controlled by numerous products that are found in local drug stores. Excessive dandruff conditions should be treated by a doctor.

Receding and Thin Hairlines Receding hairlines and thin spots can be penciled in with eyebrow pencils that match the natural color. Use the fine edge of the theatrically cut pencil; individual hairlike strokes should be applied in the direction of the natural growth of the hair.

Balding Spots These are covered by hair sprays that are color matched to the natural hair color. Part the hair away from the spot, spray carefully, and comb the hair back into place. Be sure to protect the face and wardrobe from the spray. In place of sprays, matching colors of water-soluble makeup may be dabbed over the prominent area.

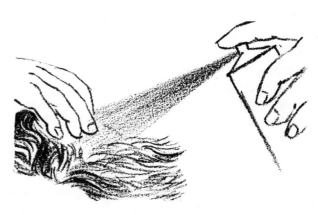

SECTION TWO REVIEW

1. With reference to skin conditioning, what treatments are used to balance (a) dry skin, (b) oily skin?
2. List the four basic skin tones. What is the simplest method used to select a base shade of makeup?
3. What types of makeup should be used if there is a skin reaction to a standard brand?
4. Describe the application and characteristics of moist rouge and shadow in contrast to dry rouge and shadow.
5. After powdering, what techniques do you use to set the makeup?
6. Using the guide for a natural brow provided in Chapter 11, sketch a pair of eyebrows free-hand.
7. What are the most complimentary shades of lipstick for people with fair complexions? With brown complexions?
8. On a chart of the face, indicate areas most commonly shaded and high-lighted when a corrective makeup is applied.
9. Discoloration on the skin is diminished by the use of specific makeup colors. What colors will correct a dark or bluish skin tone? What colors will correct a red skin tone?
10. What is the purpose of using spirit gum when making up an old scar?
11. For your picture file, collect examples of natural beauty makeups and high fashion makeups especially emphasizing the eyes.
12. From a local supplier, list the names of commercial products that will solve all the hair problems listed in the section on natural hair care.

Section Three

Character Makeup

Al Mayton

Under-base Makeup: Painting with Pastels and Grease

Chapter 15

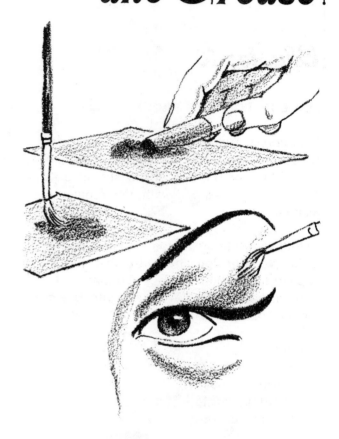

The artist should next study the technique of applying an under base. This technique will be mentioned several times in succeeding chapters. For an under base, a lighter shade of base makeup is stippled on the face before the character base color, thus neutralizing the natural skin tone. The under base should be a tone of yellow or olive. Primarily it is used to block skin color. Persons with brown complexions will use it when applying a white face, and those with fair complexions will use it when executing a dark face.

Developing a theatrical character with makeup is creating an illusionary living portrait. With prior knowledge of bone structure, research and makeup techniques, you can easily learn to develop stage characters. Basic painting and modeling of numerous individual character types will be discussed in each chapter.

Pastel coloring, a unique method for subtle shading, will be discussed now only as it generally pertains to all of the ensuing styles. A character is most strikingly emphasized by the use of highlight, shadow, and/or color. After a makeup has been completed with grease and powder, extra emphasis can be applied with soft artist's pastels. (An almost unlimited range of color is now available.)

Light natural shades can be used to bring out areas; dark natural shades can be used for depth; and rainbow colors can be used to add special or unrealistic effects. Purchase the desired color of soft pastel from any art supply store; then make it into a fine powder by rubbing it across a piece of fine sandpaper. With the use of round water-color brushes, apply the powder subtly on the area to be emphasized. You'll have to experiment with the pastels extensively to understand the color effects and to gain control of the application. Skill in the use of soft artist's pastels is mandatory before you can advance into character makeup.

Makeup and Paint for Latex Surfaces

Chapter 16

MAKEUP FOR THE FACE

Commercial Rubber Grease This is excellent for covering any latex or rubber already applied to the face or body. A shade should be purchased to correspond with the regular base makeup.

Self-mixed Rubber Grease This is a self-made makeup cover for any latex that has been applied to the body or face. To match regular base makeup, it is developed with the same (grease) base makeup.

Formula:
      Base makeup (grease or oil base)
      Castor oil (heavy)
      Powder (translucent or tinted)
      Spatula, palette

Into an amount of makeup base sufficient to execute several regular makeups, add several drops of castor oil to make a creamy paste. Blend the two ingredients with a spatula until all the lumps have disappeared. Next add several shakes of powder for opacity and combine with makeup. If the rubber grease makeup appears to be too thick, it can be thinned with alcohol. If too small an amount of castor oil is used, the makeup will lighten as time passes; if there is too much, coverage will be insufficient.

A BASIC COLORING AGENT

This material is generally known as a universal-type colorant for tinting such materials as latex, alkyd, acrylic, poly vynal acetate, and oleoresinous paints. It is sold at local paint stores and packaged in highly concentrated forms. In general, do not use more than 6 to 10 percent when tinting latex or paint. *Recommended colors:* A basic collection includes red, blue, yellow, burnt sienna, burnt umber, raw sienna, raw umber, black, and white. A brown-red, if available, may be used for skin tone, or you can slowly mix red, yellow, raw sienna, or raw umber into a white base for the same purpose.

SELF-MIXED LATEX PAINT

This paint is used for highly flexible masks, pre-applied prosthetics, and latex props, and also for scenery. *Do not* apply this to the face or body. With this formula, latex objects will withstand extreme bending and stretching.

Formula:
      Rubber cement (base)
      Benzol (thinner)
      Color (select one): Japan color, dry powder
            color, or oil-base art stroke color

For brushing, add color to two parts rubber cement and thin with one part benzol; for spraying, gradually add more thinner until the spray gun flows freely. Clean up with benzol, being careful to avoid contact with the skin. Several coats may be needed for complete opacity. Allow each coat to dry before applying another. Benzol causes expansion in latex, but the latex will return to its original shape when dry. Powder the final coat.

Individual Makeup Effects

Chapter 17

Section 3 deals mainly with the major styles of character makeup. Following are many techniques that can be used individually or incorporated into a character makeup.

BASIC DERMA WAX APPLICATION

Wax is a versatile product. Not only is it fast to use, but it can be shaped into many different forms. It is not advisable to use it on areas of the face that will be extremely mobile, because wax has little flexibility. It is excellent on areas that are to remain relatively stable. You can use it for cuts, stylized noses, covering, swelling, etc.

Materials:
    Red pencil
    Derma wax
    Base makeup
    Spirit gum
    Cotton
    Modeling tools
    Hairstyling gel

Application:
1. Draw a red pencil line around the area to be sculpted. Try to stay within the pattern, because uncontrolled modeling has a tendency to expand over too large an area.

Character Makeup

2. Paint the skin within this area with spirit gum; before it dries, touch it with loose cotton so that small fibers will protrude.

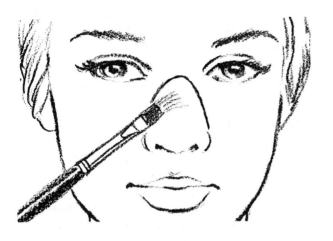

3. To color the wax, mix a small amount of base makeup into it and mix together with a spatula. In general, only a small amount of wax is needed.

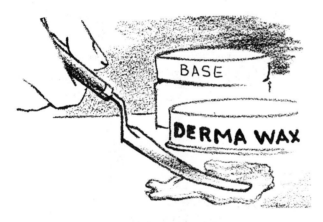

4. Press the wax onto the skin; the small cotton fibers will help the wax to adhere.

5. Put hairstyling gel on your fingers; then with the gel and modeling tools, start to develop the shape, smoothing it out. All wax edges must be blended into the skin.

6. When the shape is complete and the gel has dried, stipple the wax with a stiff brush for texture.

7. Spray the wax with medical spray or stipple plastic sealer; dry, powder, brush off the excess, and makeup.
8. If wax is used on a mobile area of the face to create a simple prosthetic, it will maintain its shape longer if, after modeling, a thin coat of liquid latex is stippled over the wax and slightly onto the skin. Dry the latex, powder, and brush off the excess; follow step 7 above or make up over the latex with rubber grease makeup.

NOSE

Use the technique for applying wax:

Broken This is created with a small mound of wax (placed two-thirds of the way up and on the side of the nose). It should be modeled to extend outward and upward to show in profile. When making up, highlight and shadow must be used to accentuate the injury.

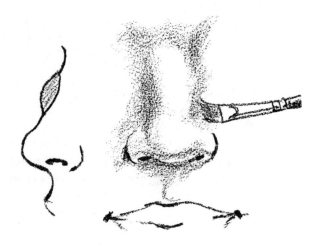

Extended See diagram.

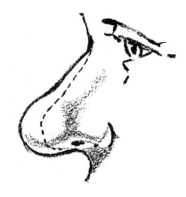

Character See diagram.

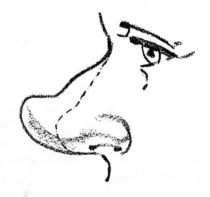

After applying the base makeup, highlight, and shadow, lightly stipple the entire nose with brown, brownish-red, red, or any lining color that compliments the character. The final stipple breaks up the flatness caused by heavy base application. For greater durability, these pieces should be constructed from latex.

NOSE PLUGS

To help simulate a broken nose or flared nostrils, use nose plugs constructed from clear, flexible plastic tubing. Hollow tubing is used to allow free breathing. Select the proper diameter of tubing that will comfortably fit into the nostril. Slice a section of tubing ⅛ to ¼ inch thick. To accentuate the broken nose, place the plug in the nostril opposite the break.

EYEBROW BLOCKOUT

1. To eradicate the eyebrow, work enough wax into the hair so that the eyebrow lies flat against the frontal bone. Spirit gum lightly painted across the eyebrow hair and pressed down is another technique, but the gum is difficult to remove.

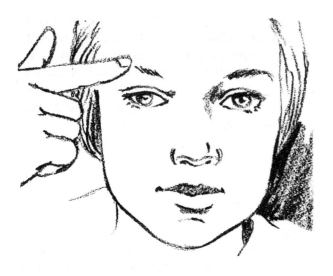

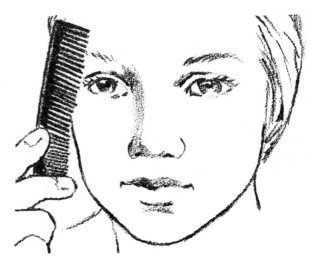

2. After the eyebrow hair has been firmly pressed down, stipple it with theatrical sealer or surgical spray dressing. Be sure to cover the eyes and nose when spraying around the face.

BODY PAINT FOR DESIGNS

The painting of pictures and designs on the body has been difficult, because movement causes cracking and peeling. Two types of paint for this purpose, which can be purchased in local art stores, are nontoxic plastic vinyl or acrylic. They paint easily, can be retouched, and wash off with soap and water.

CUTS AND SCARS

Pencil A quick scar can be drawn over the base makeup with a brown and red pencil. Draw the scar in red (for soreness), then draw with dark brown next to it. Remember that a scar or cut is an irregular break of the skin: do not draw a straight, unnatural-looking line. The colors used in creating a bruise can also be used in conjunction with a cut or scar to denote swelling or infection. Additional color is important to achieve the correct illusion.

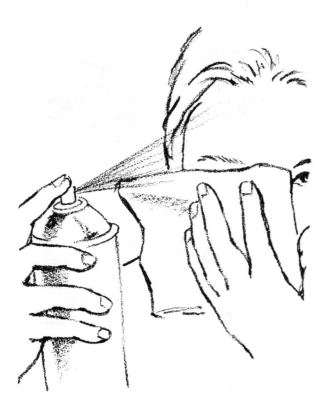

3. Allow to dry, then powder; cover over with a light base makeup or under base; powder again, and continue with character makeup.
4. For removal, wax can be combed out, but gum must be removed with either alcohol or Clens makeup remover.

Wax or Putty This scar or cut should be applied before the makeup.

1. With a red pencil draw the direction of the scar to be applied.

2. Follow general directions for basic derma wax application.
3. Model the wax so that the highest part is in the center of the scar, each end has a taper, and the edges blend into the skin. This can be accomplished with small wooden modeling tools and the fingers.

4. The application of hairstyling gel to the fingers while modeling gives you better control over the wax.
5. After the gel has evaporated, stipple the wax with a very stiff brush; this will simulate pore structure and eliminate the smooth waxy appearance.

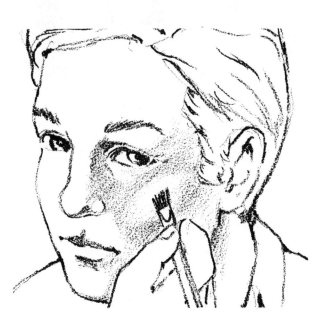

6. Open the wax with the pointed tool (remember not to make a straight line), fold back, and break the edges at irregular intervals.

Character Makeup

7. Paint the wax scar with a coat of sealer or spray bandage, allowing each to dry; powder and brush off the excess.
8. Makeup
   a. Cover the cut or scar with the base makeup.
   b. Fresh cuts have little discoloration around them; to create older scars refer to the makeup description for bruises. Very old scars are lighter due to healing.

   c. Color inside the cut with dark brown and red liner.

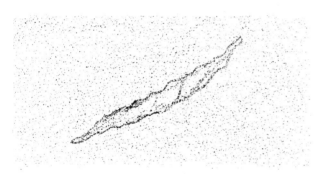

   d. Highlight the edges of the cut with white liner or a light base color. Use light pinks and lavender to makeup and color old scars.

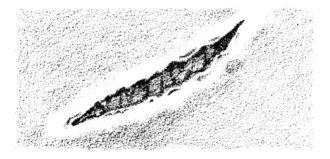

   e. Blend all colors for naturalness.
   f. Add blood if necessary (discussed below).

Latex

1. Separate a single sheet of tissue.
2. Tear a strip of tissue from the sheet, making sure the edges are ragged. The torn strip must be longer than the planned scar and ½ inch wide.
3. Apply the tissue to the face with the use of liquid latex. Mold the saturated tissue into the desired shape; open it down the center and push back the sides at irregular widths. This must all be accomplished while the latex is wet.

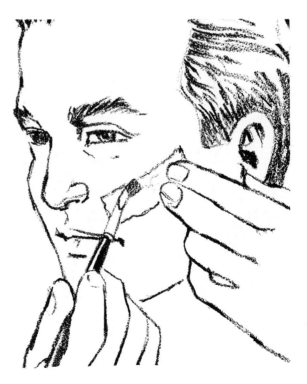

4. Dry, powder, cover with spray bandage, and make up with a rubber color that matches the base. As previously recommended, make up with highlighting, shadow, and/or colors.

5. If carefully removed, the latex scar may be reused in future performances.

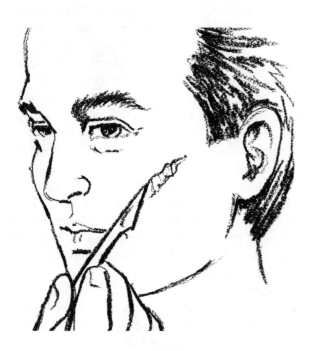

BRUISES

A bruise is an area of swelling with the center being the lightest because it is the puffiest; the discoloration becomes deeper as it graduates to the outside edges.

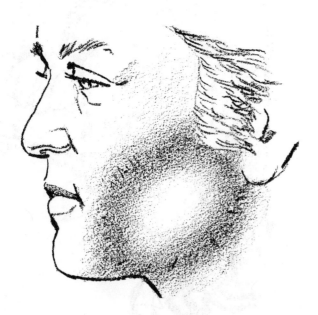

Materials:
Stipple sponge—one for each color
Lining colors—white, yellow, lavender, maroon, or vermilion
Additional lining colors—gray, blue, green
Translucent powder and puff

Application:
1. Apply and finish the makeup base. Locate the area for the bruise.
2. In the center of the projected swelling, stipple with white or a highlight color.

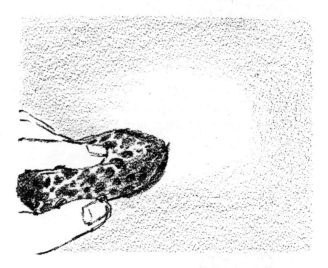

3. Next, stipple yellow liner, making the area a little larger but not covering the white center and not forming a circle.

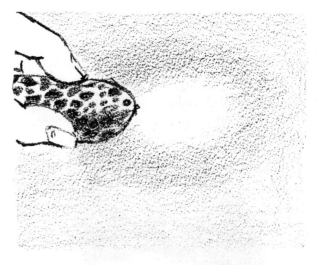

4. Stipple lavender, again overlapping and blending with the yellow but not completely

Character Makeup

covering. Additional colors may be added at this time.

5. Powder and brush off the excess powder.
6. Stipple maroon or vermilion liner over the entire bruise, powder, and remove excess powder with a damp sponge.

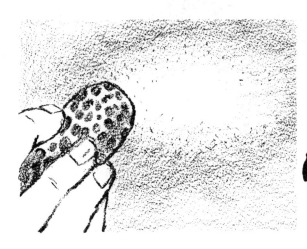

7. In a black eye, discoloration usually appears on the lid, in the socket area, and underneath. A red pencil can be applied to the table of the eye to add a finishing touch for soreness.

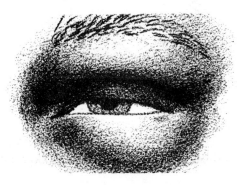

8. To add a shine to the discoloration, lightly dab it with cocoa butter, or stipple it with glycerine.

BLOOD

Theatrical blood may be purchased, but it can be simulated from local products. Use caution in selecting red materials because many are toxic and highly staining. Two recommended products are children's red finger paint, which is somewhat washable, or a mixture of oil and liner. Melt 1½ teaspoons of vermilion (red) liner and 2 ounces of baby oil or olive oil in a heat-resistant glass container. A small amount of brown or dark blue grease may be added for color correction. If the mixture has a tendency to thicken, warm it and add a little more oil.

"Nextel" simulated blood is a nonstaining theatrical makeup designed for realism on the stage as well as film. It can easily be removed from the skin or costumes with water.

BURNS

Burns can be simulated in about the same manner as cuts and scars, using either wax or latex.

Materials:

Liners—brown, vermilion or red, black, white

Spray bandage or plastic sealer

Vaseline petroleum jelly

Water-soluble makeup or poster color—black

Stipple sponge—one for each color

Application:

1. First-degree burns: These are created by contrasting areas of skin. The burned portion is simulated with red and brown liner stippled, powdered, and damp-sponged. Surrounding areas should be pale to simulate shock.

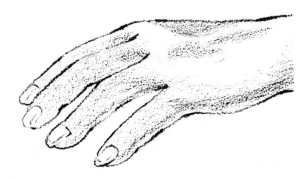

2. Second-degree burns: Stipple with the same colors listed for first-degree burns, but apply color more heavily and add blisters.

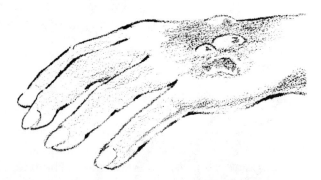

3. Third-degree burns: These are the most severe. Follow the techniques for first- and second-degree burns. In addition, irregularly stipple around the burn with black water-soluble makeup or poster color to simulate dry, cracked skin.

BLISTERS

These are simulated with either broken or raised areas of skin usually in conjunction with burns and bruises.

Broken Blisters

1. Make up as for a first-degree burn.
2. Stipple a coat of latex over it and dry.
3. Before powdering, carefully lift the latex center and break it to the desired size of the blister.

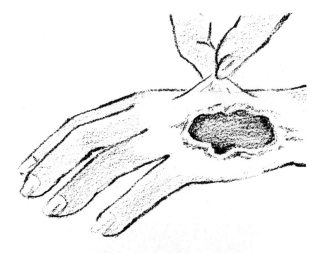

4. Make up and stipple the latex with a rubber base makeup that matches the skin tone or is slightly tinged with red; powder and set.

Character Makeup

5. Paint Vaseline petroleum jelly or baby oil inside the blister for soreness.

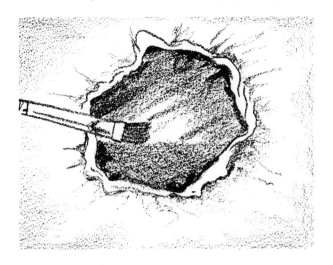

Raised Blisters
1. Spatula a dome of yellow-tinted Vaseline or wax onto the skin.

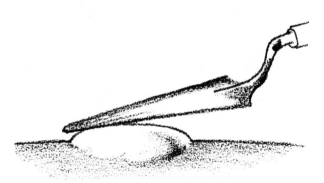

2. Spray it with a coat of medical spray bandage, dry, powder, and blot carefully with a damp sponge.
3. Make up around the blister with base makeup and stipple with the colors used for a second-degree burn.

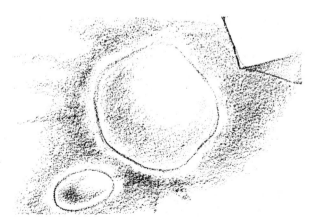

PERSPIRATION

For the most long-lasting appearance of a sweaty condition, use glycerine. It can be stippled on the face, full strength, with a stipple sponge or sprayed after being mixed with water in an atomizer (2½ parts glycerine to 1 part water).

TEARS

At times it is necessary to create tears. Ammonia capsules can be hidden in the palm of the hand or in a handkerchief. On cue, the capsule is broken with a squeeze of the fingers and carefully passed beneath the nose. The rising fumes will cause the eyes to tear. To simulate a tear or tear-streaked cheek, glycerine can be applied with the tip of a brush handle.

UNSHAVEN EFFECT WITH MAKEUP

A five o'clock shadow or several days' growth can be created with makeup or small pieces of hair. Both methods are quite effective. The final result will be an even-textured "growth" within the confines of a man's natural beard or hair line.

Materials:
    Stipple sponge—one for each color
    Base makeup
    Powder and puff
    White rubber sponge
    Liners or makeup colors—dark brown and
        black

Application:
1. Apply the base color and powder.
2. Mix the dark brown makeup with the black in a ratio of 2 to 1. Tap the stipple sponge on the makeup and then touch it to the heel of the hand to remove any excess. Each time the sponge is tapped onto the makeup, be sure to remove the excess, or a dark spot may develop. These spots are difficult to remove without causing the makeup to appear messy.

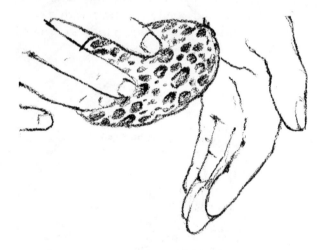

3. With a light touch, apply it to the face following the natural beard line.

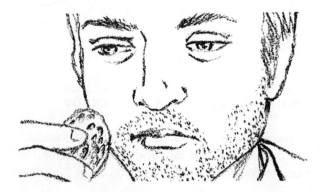

4. To deepen the shadow, powder the first application, remove excess powder, and lightly stipple a darker brown or black over it. This layer must also be powdered and damp-sponged.
5. Excessive stippling can create an even color that looks artificial and thereby loses its desired effect.

If the beard is too dark or some spots appear too dark, powder and lighten it by stippling over with a little of the original base color on a clean sponge.

TOOTH DISCOLORATION

When possible, use the device of tooth aging to help develop an aged character. I strongly warn the actor, however, not to use any artificial colors on false teeth or on caps, because permanent staining can occur.

Materials:
    Facial tissue
    Brown and/or yellow liner
    Brown pencil or black tooth enamel
    Spirit gum

Application:
1. Open the mouth and dry the teeth with a tissue. The mouth must remain open and dry throughout the entire procedure. Cotton may be placed between the lips and gums to absorb saliva.

Character Makeup

2. With brown and yellow liner or brown eyebrow pencil, mark and discolor the teeth. Fill areas between the teeth with dark brown, color irregularly along the edge to break up the straight line.

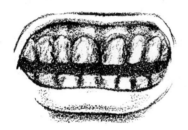

3. Powder lightly with a brush.
4. Over the color, paint a thin coat of spirit gum. *Caution:* Do not allow wet spirit gum to transfer from the teeth to the inside of the mouth.

5. The mouth should be closed, and no food can be eaten. Food causes the spirit gum to wear off, making it necessary to redo the process.
6. Theatrical tooth enamel may also be used, but the colors are limited. For extreme contrast, black is available. If teeth are naturally discolored, white and lighter shades of enamel will brighten them. To remove the tooth discoloration following a performance, rub the teeth firmly with a dry cloth.

GOLD OR SILVER TEETH

1. Dry the tooth, as explained in preceeding *Application.*
2. Separate the metal from gold- or silver-foil-wrapped gum or candy; or purchase imitation gold leaf from an art store.
3. Paint the tooth with spirit gum. Again you are reminded that this must not be done on caps or false teeth.
4. With a pair of tweezers, hold the metal foil to the tooth and lightly tap tooth with a soft makeup brush; then press gently to create a more secure bond.

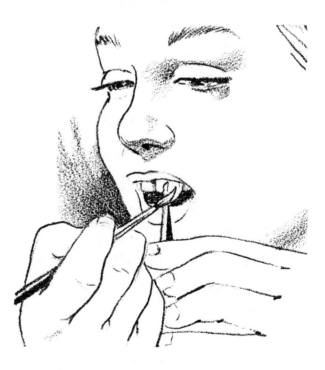

5. Eating and drinking should be avoided, since the foil can easily come off in the process.

1. In order that the tattoos will match at every performance, sketch the original design in reverse with a soft lead pencil on heavy bond paper.

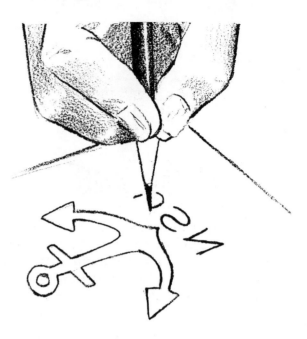

2. Over this, lay a sheet of thin tissue paper and trace the design with red or blue indelible pencils. Make as many copies as needed.

METALLIC MAKEUP

Metallic makeup is available from theatrical suppliers, but a quick technique is to cover the face with a thin coat of Vaseline petroleum jelly and dust it with metallic powder that has been pressed onto a puff. If smeared, it is easily repaired with a similar dusting. This process is not recommended for coating the entire body. Do not inhale or get the powder in the eyes. A good solvent for removing the Vaseline base is kerosene or Clens makeup remover, followed by washing with soap and water.

TATTOOS

Materials:
> Soft lead pencil and paper
> Tissue paper
> Indelible pencils—red, blue
> Water

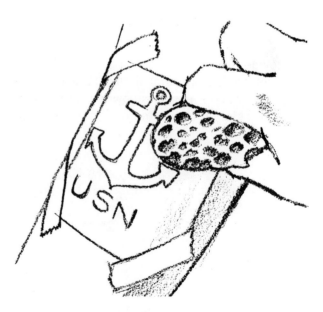

3. Place the pencil side of the indelible copy against the skin and dampen the back side with water. The design will transfer to the skin. With the pencils, lines can be sharpened up and areas filled in.

Basic White Face

Chapter 18

The basic white face is the foundation used to create such makeup as clown, horror, fantasy, and stylized illusions. The original formula, as used by circus clowns, was a mixture of powdered zinc oxide and vegetable shortening. These ingredients were thoroughly mixed into an opaque paste and applied as makeup. The more nostalgic student may want to experiment with this traditional formula.

If a makeup color other than white is needed—red, blue, etc.—apply the pure grease color as purchased; or, for a pastel effect, mix lining color into white grease with a spatula and continue with the application and techniques as outlined.

Materials:

    White makeup base (clown white)
    White powder or talcum powder
    Powder puff
    Makeup sponge, rubber
    Soft gray drafting pencil
    Lining colors (grease) or nontoxic water-soluble paint (water color or poster paint)
    Assorted brushes

Application:

1. For fair complexions, apply white grease makeup with the fingers, since the warmth from the hands aids in spreading it evenly. If the neck and ears are exposed, be sure to cover them with the base makeup. It should not be applied too thickly, and the coverage should be just sufficient to keep any skin tone from showing through. It is important to note, however, that people with brown complexions require a light under-base makeup, dominantly yellow, to block out the natural skin tone. This should be applied sparingly and powdered; then the basic white face is stippled over this foundation.

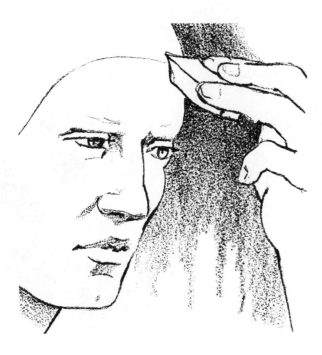

2. With the makeup sponge, continue to stipple over the applied white base to achieve a smooth finish. If a shaded effect in the character is desired, blend the lining or grease color into the applied white grease before powdering.
3. Powder makeup sufficiently to absorb all the oil, making sure to brush off excess powder; this creates a dry surface which is receptive to painted-on color and pastel shading.
4. Color application:
   a. If you are proficient at freehand drawing, sketch the outline of the pattern lightly on the face with a soft gray pencil before applying any color.
   b. With the assorted brushes, apply the chosen color, grease or water soluble.

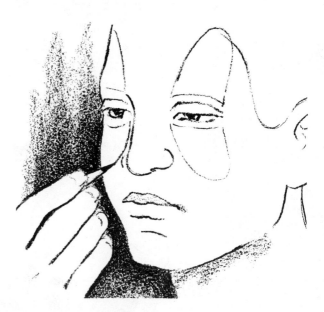

   c. After applying grease color or liner, you must powder it to prevent smearing. To eliminate smearing or unwanted blending, if two or more colors are used, each must be individually powdered before the next one is applied. To restore the original color, pat a dampened sponge over the face, thereby removing all excess powder.
   d. There is a wide range of extremely effective water-soluble colors such as liquid and cake water color, colored cosmetic eyeliners and shadows, acrylics, etc. In its dry form, the latter must be moistened before being applied. When any water-soluble product is used it must be applied thinly, because, when dry, it will crack from facial movements. Water-soluble colors should not be powdered or wet-sponged.
   e. In either case, if difficulty is encountered when applying broad areas of color over the white base, you may need to remove the white makeup within the area before applying the color.
   f. When outlining colored grease patterns, powder well, remove excess, and line with a water-soluble color.

Character Makeup

Basic Dark Face
Chapter 19

It's as easy to apply a smooth dark face as a white one, if care is taken in application. Racial types have always held relevant roles on the stage, and their correct makeup is essential.

To create the illusion of a Mexican, Indian, or Negro on someone with a fair complexion, you must apply an under base before the base color. Persons with brown complexions can deepen their skin tone by selecting base shades deeper than the natural color. After the darker base has been applied, the rules for straight and corrective makeup for brown complexions should be observed.

The following reviews some of the principles for developing the dark face and presents some additional suggestions.

Materials:
    Under-base color
    Base color
    White rubber sponge
    Puff
    Assorted brushes
    Tinted powder (amber or brown)
    Black eyebrow pencil
    Black mascara
    Black eyeliner
    Rouge (moist or liquid), coral
    Rouge, brush-on—coral, peach, or tawny
    Lipstick—coral or orange

Application:

1. Apply the under base to the face, ears, and neck with the white sponge, being careful to completely cover all exposed skin, including areas inside the ears and in the hairline.

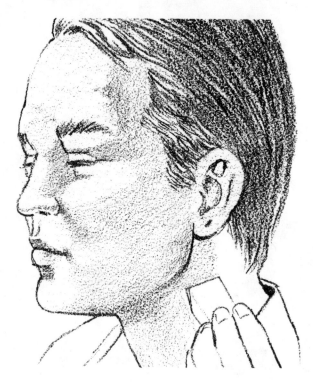

2. Stipple the darker base color of the theatrical character to be portrayed over the under base until the makeup has a smooth appearance. Use the base color generously.

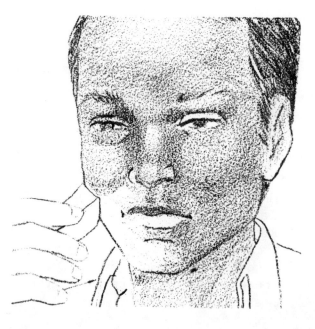

3. To emphasize particular areas of the face, highlights may be added. The highlight color should be a light base shade that is compatible with the base color, preferably on the olive side.

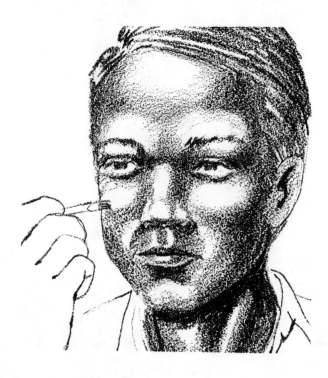

4. Apply moist or liquid rouge, either coral or orange.
5. Powder with a tinted shade, brush off excess, and pat with a damp sea sponge.
6. Line the eyes with a black pencil or liner, including the inside table of the lower lid.

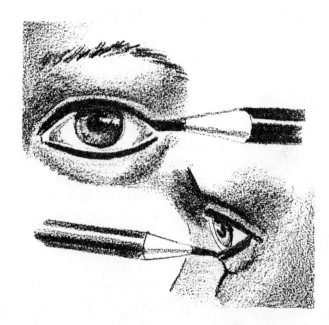

Character Makeup

7. Mascara lashes, bottom and top.
8. Dust cheeks with a peach or tawny brush-on rouge.
9. The shades of lipstick best suited for women are coral and orange; men can use the more natural shades, as suggested for natural brown complexions.
10. To eliminate a dry appearance, rub the fingers on a bar of cocoa butter and lightly pat it on the high points of the face; the cocoa butter application emits a natural shine.

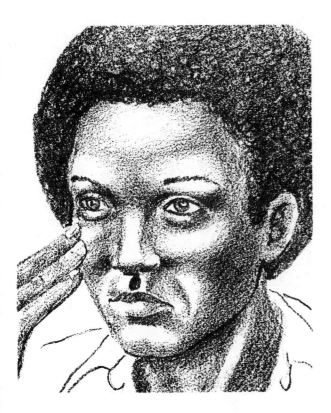

11. Body makeup:
    Apply it in the same manner as outlined in Chapter 13, selecting a shade that matches the face color.
12. Hair:
    Spray the hair black, or wear an ethnic wig.
13. What causes a dark makeup to appear spotty?
    a. The face must be kept absolutely clean and free of oil.
    b. The dark base must be applied with the stippling technique. It should be applied quickly, because over-handling will cause it to come off.

Old Age

Chapter 20

A proficient makeup artist collects many pictorial examples of aged faces. From these portraits he can become familiar with the special traits of the aging face; for example, contour, wrinkles, skin sag, and texture.

Materials:

Base makeup: A light shade—fair, olive, or shades recommended by theatrical manufacturers

Shadow: A deep shade of brown much darker than the base

Highlight: The lightest of base makeups

Powder: White baby powder or talc

Puff: White rubber sponge

Pencils: Auburn, light brown, medium brown, gray (extra colors: blue, green, and maroon)

Stipple sponge for each makeup color

Stipple colors: Liners—shades of brown, orange, maroon, pink

Dry pastels: Highlight—toast, mushroom, pale natural colors

Dry pastels: Shadow—shades of brown, gray, blue, and green

Razor blades to keep pencils sharp

Sandpaper for pastels

Assorted brushes

Body makeup

Brown-complexioned actors should coordinate base, highlight, and powder colors to lean toward the yellow side; this color is most compatible with a dark complexion. Light bases, principally containing white, will cause an undesirable ashen cast. Shadow colors should match or be darker than the natural skin tone. For a warm stipple, orange shades should be chosen in lieu of pink.

Application:

1. In the creases that signify old age, paint in the shadow color; these creases include forehead lines, squint lines around the eyes, nasal folds, and any other areas that will add depth to age. Carefully remove any shadow color that is not directly in a crease, and then powder.

2. Squint the eyes, wrinkle the forehead and nose, and apply the base color. Natural age lines will be created when the muscles have been relaxed. Continue to make up the ears and neck.

3. Powder heavily, brushing off the excess.
4. Repeat steps 2 and 3 to build up a heavy texture.
5. Repeat step 2, but *do not* powder.
6. Shadow: Depth is a common feature of the aged face. For depth, a shadow is applied to the temples, upper eye sockets, under the eyes (to create a baggy effect), bridge of the nose, hollows in cheeks, nasal labial folds, corners of the mouth, jowls, chin creases, and the sections of the neck. Blend these areas so that the edges are very soft as they diminish into the base color. Depending on the size of the stage and the effect desired, deeper shadows may be applied with the dry pastels.

7. Highlight: This will be applied where bone or flesh is protruding or sagging. With the highlight, paint in areas such as thin lines under the forehead wrinkles, frontal bones, length of nose, bags under the eyes,

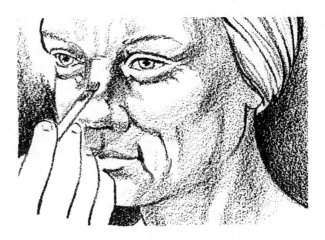

cheeks to nasal folds, cheekbones, upper lip, point of chin, and the high points of the neck. Softly blend the edges of the highlight color, but do not combine it into the shadow. One of the most important secrets of creating a good old-age makeup is perfecting the art of blending.

8. Pucker the lips and stipple them with base color.

9. Powder the entire face and remove excess.
10. Dry pastel or rouge: Highlights and shadows can now be strengthened by the use of dry colors. Interesting effects can be achieved with the use of greens and blues along with shades of brown and gray in the shadow areas. Light, dry pastels brushed across the high points of highlighted areas can define old age even more.
11. With very sharp multicolored pencils, re-strengthen the lines and wrinkles that typify aging. A light, subtle touch is necessary to prevent the look of artificially drawn lines on the face. This is achieved by using colors other than black and dark brown. The more colors that are used, the more natural the lines appear. See recommended pencil shades. The penciling is applied with broken lines into forehead creases, eye squints, nose creases, upper and lower mouth, fronts of cheeks, and around the ears and neck.

12. Stippling: For an aged skin texture, use a stipple sponge and the suggested lining colors. These are individually stippled over the face, ears, and neck. Maroon is especially reserved for the nose, cheeks, and

forehead. Be careful not to push too hard or the maroon will create a heavy spot. If a spot does occur, it can be eliminated by stippling with the base color. Overlap the colors artfully, touching the sponge to the back of the hand to remove excess makeup before applying it to the face. If desired for a final touch, stipple the entire face lightly with a highlight color. The light dots of color create the effect of rough skin.

13. Hair color: Color the hair with white or gray hair spray. If the natural hair is too dark, it many need spraying with a yellow or blond shade before the white one. Brush some of it onto the eyebrows and eyelashes. After coloring the brows, you can glue white or gray crepe wool over them for additional effect. Remember to protect the face when using any type of spray material.

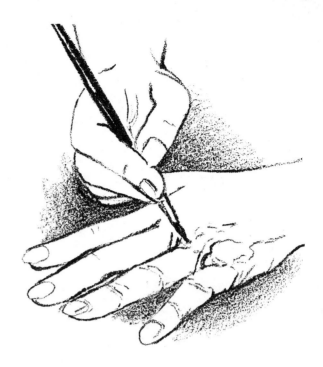

Optional Effects:

1. Aging the teeth (see Chapter 17).
2. Aging the hands:
   a. Cover the hands and nails with a matching base color, preferably using a water-soluble makeup.
   b. Between the fingers and up onto the backs of the hand, lightly paint shadow colors with a brush and soften the edges by blending. On the high points of the fingers and the knuckles, apply a highlight and blend.

c. Stipple the same colors used on the face to the back of the hands; powder, and remove the excess.
d. Discolor the fingernails with a brown eyebrow pencil; mark them up and smudge the color.

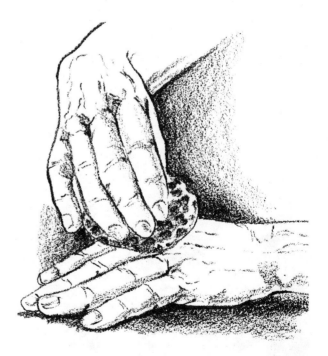

3. Wigs: White or gray, styled for period.
4. Wax: With the use of wax, extend the nose downward before making up.

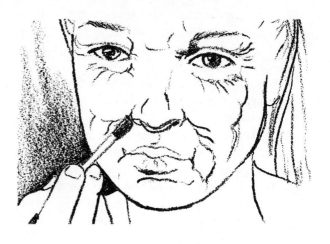

Spray Bandage: Do not spray it around the eyes or up into the nostrils; in these areas, spray the material into a container and apply it with a brush. To keep the material from shining, powder it immediately after application.

ADVANCED TECHNIQUES

Latex Wrinkles Apply a thin coat of grease makeup to the face, then powder. Next, stretch the individual areas of the skin, stipple it with liquid latex, dry thoroughly, powder, and release. The more times the above process is repeated, the more the wrinkles will increase in depth. Next, coat it with plastic sealer or surgical spray bandage before makeup—unless rubber grease makeup is used

Latex wrinkles are extremely effective but hard to remove. Be sure to avoid getting latex into the eyebrows, eyelashes, and, especially, the eyes; cover the brows with wax if necessary. Latex will not harm the skin unless there is an allergy; test latex on the forearm for several hours, before applying it to the face, to see if there is a reaction. Clens makeup remover works very well on latex.

Rubberized Cotton and Tissue Appliances

1. As before, first make up the face with a thin coat of grease makeup and powder; this will later act as a release agent for the dried latex.
2. Saturate small amounts of cotton with latex and mold into place, feathering out the

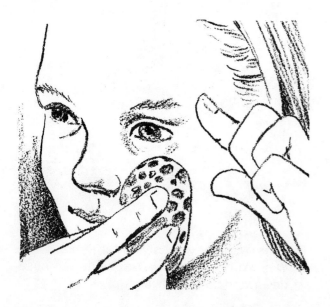

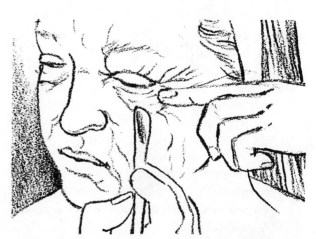

Character Makeup

edges of the cotton to lie against the face. With this technique, extra features such as bags, jowls, nasal folds, etc., can be constructed.

3. Separate a single sheet of facial tissue, making it as thin as possible; tear all edges until they are uneven; apply the tissue to the face by stippling with liquid latex. Cover the entire face, including the applications of cotton, according to this procedure.

Here are some points to remember when working with latex:

1. Rubberized facial tissue and cotton quickly lose elasticity and should not be used for areas of great stress such as the mouth.
2. Liquid latex should have the consistency of eyelash adhesive; distilled water may be added to aging or thickening latex.
3. Take off latex from the skin with Clens makeup remover; an ice cube rubbed on the latex can promote the separation.

4. Dry the latex and powder.
5. Make up the face as customary for an aged makeup. Use rubber grease makeup for a base, if possible, or coat the dried latex with plastic sealer or surgical spray bandage.

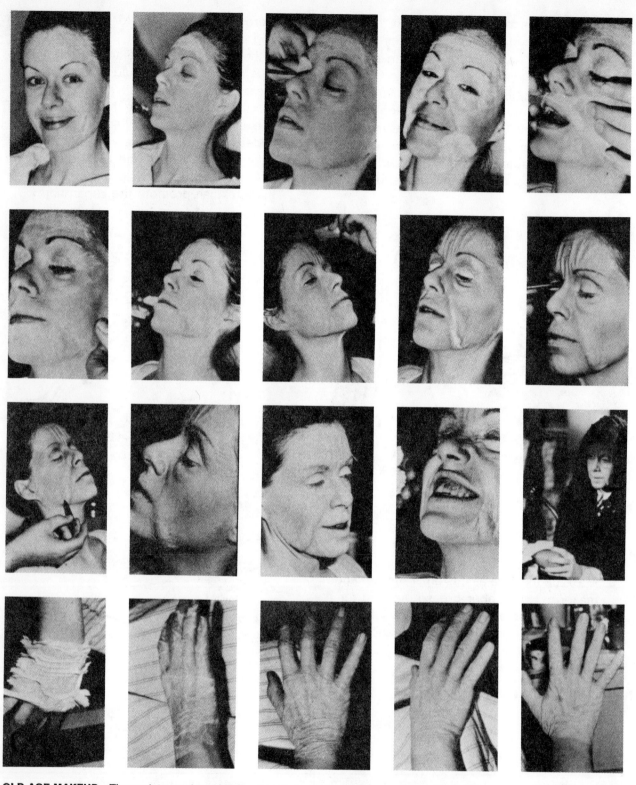

OLD-AGE MAKEUP   These pictures show an old-age makeup created by the author on Virginia Scott ·King for a TeleKETiCS Film produced by the Franciscan Communication Center.

The first phase included adhering a pair of preformed latex eyebags (prosthetics). Jowels were sculpted on the cheeks using modeling wax. Liquid latex and wrinkled tissue were applied to the forehead and eyelids. Over the entire face and neck, while stretching the skin, two layers of liquid latex were stippled. Each layer was dried and powdered.

The second phase consisted of applying the rubber grease foundation, blending in highlights and shadows, then powdering again. Additional accents were added with dry pastels, multicolored pencil lines, and an overall stippling with brown and maroon liner, on a coarse sponge, for a rough skin texture.

Phase three completed the face: false eyebrows, hair coloring, teeth, and maroon eye lining.

Phase four consisted of aging the hands; liquid latex and wrinkled tissue were applied to the backs of the hands and fingers. After drying, the techniques of phase two were used; then the fingernails were darkened and age spots were painted on the hands with a brown gel makeup.

Oriental

Chapter 21

The Oriental illusion can be skillfully created with grease makeup only, but for a more advanced approach, the addition of clear-type adhesive will heighten the effect. The following techniques are valuable in developing all types of Oriental characters, both natural and traditional.

Materials:
Base makeup—yellowish-brown undertone
Highlight—white grease

Shadow—soft brown grease or dry shadow (pastels)
White rubber sponge
Puff
Powder—translucent or white
Lipstick—brown tones of pink and coral or red
Black eyeliner
Black eyebrow pencil
Black mascara
Black false eyelashes
Dry rouge—amber or pink
Assorted liners or colored grease

Application:

1. If you plan to include the tape technique, apply it before starting the makeup. When Oriental makeup is worn by a man, the eyebrows should be half covered, working in from the outside; the illusion can be further enhanced if the artist creates an upward brow with pencil or crepe wool.

2. Base makeup: Select a color that has a yellowish-brown undertone such as olive or theatrical Chinese. The depth of color will be determined by the type of character, lighting, and the size of the theater. Apply the base over the entire face, neck, and ears with a white rubber sponge. If geisha makeup is desired, begin with a white base and powder, eliminating steps 3 and 4. When creating the traditional Chinese theater character, colors must be applied as outlined in Chapter 18 on the white face.

3. Highlight: Mix a small amount of the base makeup with white grease and apply it around the eyes (top and bottom), the sides

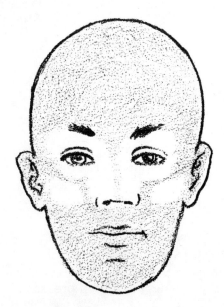

of the nose, and the high cheekbones. Softly blend the highlight with the base color.

4. Shadow: To add height to the cheekbones, a soft warm shadow can be applied in the hollows of the cheeks and subtly blended outward; this can be applied with brown grease before the powdering or with an amber dry rouge after the makeup has been set.

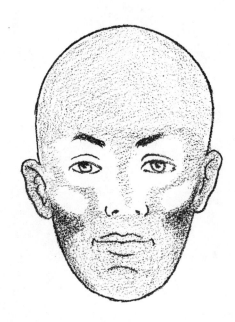

5. Powder sufficiently, brush off the excess, and blot with a damp sponge.

6. Eyeliner: To create the almond eye, use a fine brush to draw a line across the edge of the inner eye, painting directly over the tape if it has been used; extend the line along the lid and lift it slightly on the outside corner. Back at the inside corner, a thin white line drawn next to the black one will create greater contrast. Depending upon the size of the theater, a lower line may not be necessary; but, if needed, it can be applied in varying degrees. The proce-

Character Makeup

dure is to connect the lower line at the inside corner of the eye, extend it under the lower lashes, and reconnect it with the upper line in a rising motion or leave a separation.

7. Eyebrows: Pencil them with the black eyebrow pencil, creating small hairline strokes. Avoid drawing the brow down or making it too heavy on the outside. If the brow is at least half-way blocked out, it is simple to resketch it sparsely, and at an upward angle.

8. Lashes: Use a light wisp of black mascara across the lashes, or, depending on the character, an appropriate thickness of false lashes.

9. Dry rouge: For added tone, use a color such as amber in the hollows of the cheeks, but if the character is a geisha, lightly use pink on the cheeks and around the eyes.

10. Lipstick: For women, brown tones of pink or coral are most applicable, but reds are traditional for a geisha. In either case, the mouth should be painted small. Lipstick for men is not usually needed, but the natural tones can be used for accenting.

11. Body makeup: Matching tones of water-soluble makeup should be used for the body makeup.

12. Hair: Use a stylized Oriental black wig, or spray the hair black. To further develop an Oriental character for men, stylized moustaches, chin beards, and bald caps may be incorporated into the makeup.

ADVANCED ORIENTAL TECHNIQUES

Materials:

Clear adhesive tape—one inch
Scissors
Heavy black thread and a needle
Tweezers

The Inner Eye Tab

Construction: A quick and effective Oriental illusion can be made with clear tape cut in the shape of a crescent moon; the tape is placed with tweezers so as to cover the inside corner of the eye. The diagram indicates the approximate size and shape and may be used as a pattern. For extremely large or small eyes, the pattern will have to be modified.

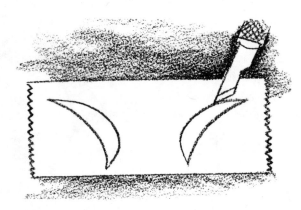

Application:

1. Remove all oil from the area around the inside corners of the eyes.
2. After cutting out the desired shape, hold the top point with the end of the tweezers. Avoid touching the sticky portion of the tape with the fingers or it will lose its adhesive qualities.

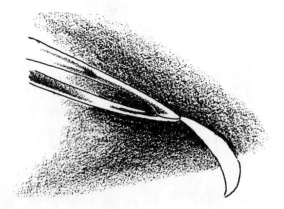

3. With the eye slightly open, place the crescent tape at an angle so that the top point will lie along the upper lid and lashes while the lower point extends below and covers the inside corner of the eye.

4. Press it firmly into place. Assistance may be needed to place the tape at the proper angle to the eye; correct placement requires much patience and practice.
5. With the tape in place, continue to follow the outline for an Oriental makeup. The crescent points will prevent the eyes from opening fully and the actor should use this restriction to augment his characterization.

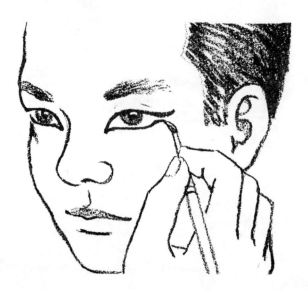

Character Makeup

The Outer Eye Tab

Construction: A triangle made from 1-inch clear tape is an advanced device that is hidden within the hair or under a wig. Cut a 3-inch strip of tape, fold one end over ½ inch, then fold the same end ½ inch more. According to the diagram cut the tape into the prescribed triangle shape, *Y:Z* being the folded end. Thread a needle with a 15-inch length of heavy black thread and sew it securely to end *Z* in the approximate area of the black dot.

Application:
1. Wipe the area around the temples with an astringent to remove excess oil.
2. In applying the tape, the entire piece should be at a slightly upward angle; point *X* should be close to the eye, and points *Y:Z* should extend partially over the hairline. Firmly press the sticky portion of the tape onto the skin.

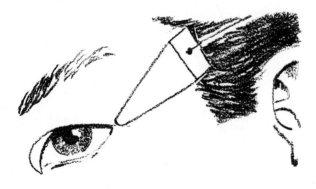

3. To hide the black thread, part the hair with a tail comb; starting at the eye tabs and going up in the direction of the crown of the head, place the thread along the scalp at an upward angle. Pull thread, applying pressure to the tape, and automatically the illusion of an Oriental will appear; do not pull tightly, however, because this tends to create wrinkles. At the crown of the head, tie the strings in a simple overhand knot, place two bobby pins at crossed angles for securing, and cut off the excess. Replace the hair by lightly combing to prevent disturbing the threads.

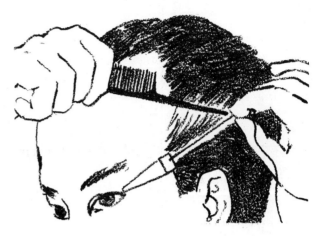

4. If further coverage is needed to disguise the tape edges, they may be stippled with liquid latex, dried, powdered, and made up with rubber grease makeup.

5. The makeup application can now be completed by covering over the tape with the desired base color and finishing as usual. If necessary, color area *Y:Z* with black makeup, then color the hair black and style it forward to aid in disguising the tape. An easier way to hide the end tape and the thread is to use a stylized Oriental wig. A new set of tabs, both inner and outer, will be needed for each performance because they lose most of their adhesive quality when removed.

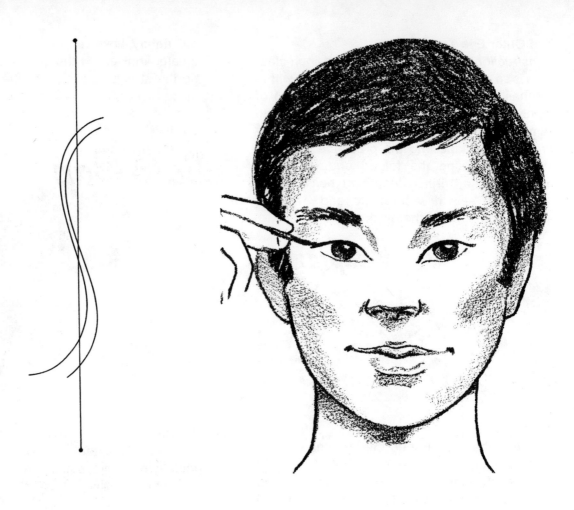

Bald Cap

Chapter 22

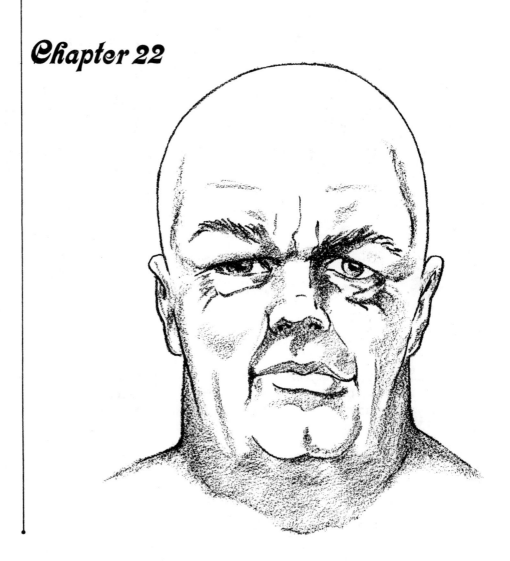

A complete balding effect is brought about by a plastic or latex cap, either purchased in a novelty store or from some professional source or personally constructed with liquid latex. The cap should fit snugly and completely to cover all the hair. The professional bald cap is constructed of a durable plastic. It is placed on the head, trimmed to fit, and glued down in the same manner as the latex cap.

Materials:
  Styrofoam wig block
  Material for papier-mâché
  (Newspaper, fine sandpaper, white glue,
    shellac)
  Scissors
  White latex sponge or a 1-inch utility brush
  1 pint liquid latex
  Latex color—pale orange or flesh tone

Construction of the Head Block:

1. Purchase a styrofoam head or wig block slightly smaller than the head size of the actor to wear the bald cap. The form must be completely smooth because all irregularities on the original block will be visible in the final product if not corrected.

2. A simple way to construct a smooth block is to cover the styrofoam head with three even coats of papier-mâché. Tear newspaper into 1½-inch squares and soak them in a solution of 4 parts glue to 1 part water for one-half hour to make them flexible.

After soaking the newspaper strips apply them to the head block, overlapping edges as they are smoothed down. Allow each

coat to dry thoroughly before you apply the next. With fine sandpaper reduce any rough

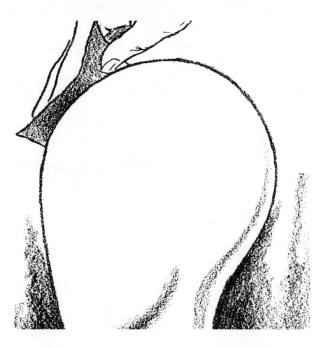

edges, and paint the head with a coat of shellac. Be sure to thin the shellac sufficiently, or the drying time will be prolonged. Fine sanding and shellacking should be repeated several times to make the block appear as smooth as glass. Allow the shellac to dry completely after each application.

3. Spray paint the papier-mâché block with several thin coats of a fast-drying silver enamel.

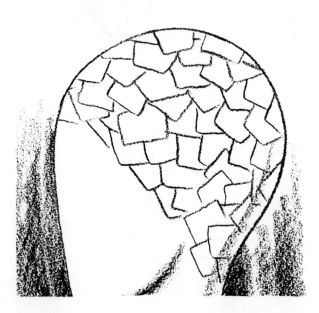

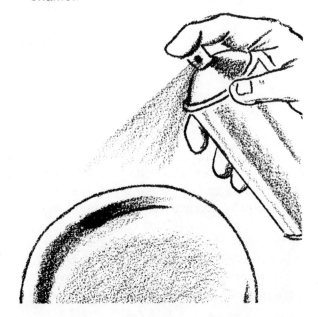

Character Makeup

Construction of the Latex Cap:

1. Color the liquid latex with a small amount of latex color, which can usually be purchased in regular paint stores. Because most colors are highly concentrated, you'll only need a fraction of a drop of color. Remember that liquid latex always dries darker than it appears when wet.

2. Over the silver enamel block, stipple two coats of colored latex and allow each to dry. Paint and individually dry six more layers,

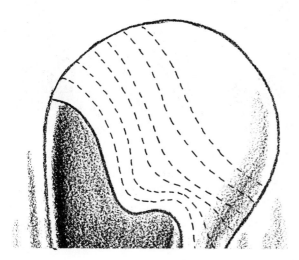

but leave a 1-inch margin with each successive coat. The outside edges of the finished bald cap, which are glued to the face and neck, should be very thin. It will require some calculation and experimentation to discover where this edge will appear.

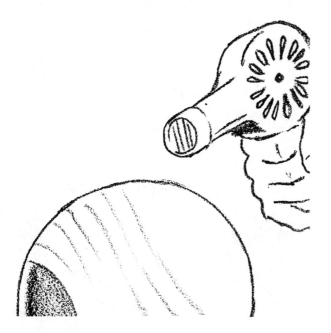

3. As previously mentioned, allow each stippled or painted coat of liquid latex to dry. Drying time of each layer may be shortened by the use of circulating warm heat from a portable hair dryer.

4. When the latex has dried, powder the entire head. Carefully lift the edges with a wooden tool; powder underneath. If the powdering instructions are not followed correctly, the edges may stick together. After all of the underneath edges have been powdered, slowly remove the cap from the block and continue to powder underneath. Shake out the excess powder. The cap is now ready for application.

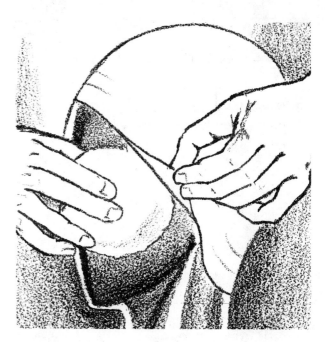

Materials:

Scissors
Red pencil
Spirit gum and brush
Plastic sealer or spray bandage
Powder and puff
White latex sponge
Base makeup or rubber grease makeup

Application:

1. Normally, the latex cap should slide directly on the uncovered head; but if the hair is too long or unruly, the head will have to be covered with a stocking cap prior to the latex one.

Bald Cap

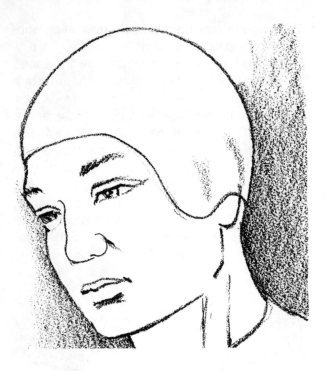

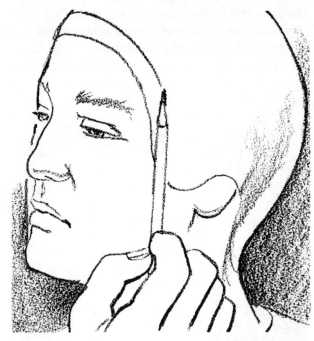

2. If novelty-store caps do not fit perfectly, the edges may be secured with clear medical tape.

b. Cut the cap with scissors along this line.
c. If the cap is too small, you'll have to make another on a larger head block; if the cap is too large, it may be filled out with facial tissue stuffed under it.

Adhering:
When the novelty-store cap, professional plastic cap, or self-constructed latex cap fits properly, spirit gum is used to fasten it to the head.
1. Always allow the spirit gum to become tacky before it finally adheres to the skin.
2. Glue the front edge down carefully, starting at the forehead.

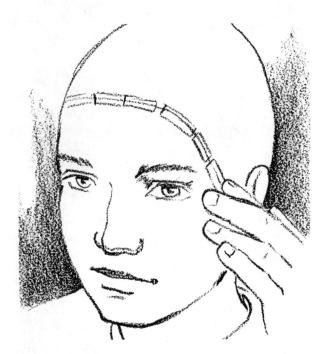

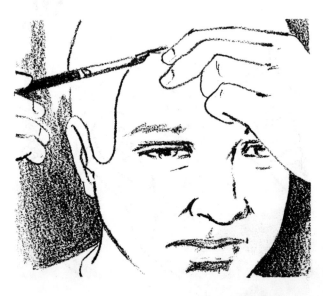

3. With the self-constructed cap on the subject's head:
a. Draw a line with a red pencil all the way around the cap. The line should run slightly below the hair line and continue around the ears.

Character Makeup

3. Glue the sides down in front of the ears separately; do not over-stretch them or they will work loose eventually.

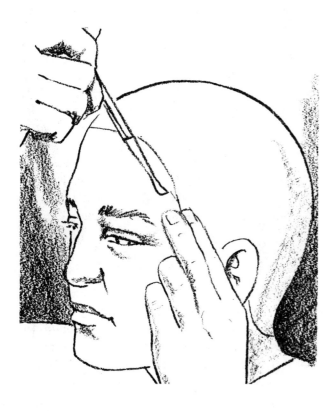

4. Tilt the head slightly backward and glue the back edge down to the neck; this procedure will produce a smooth fit.

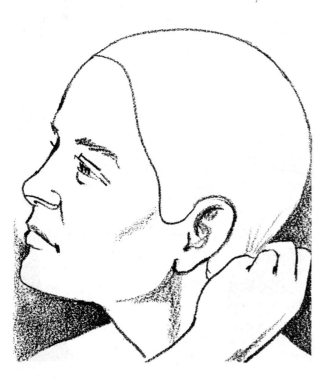

5. Glue the sides down separately in back of the ears.

Edge Blending:

1. Any visible edges can be eliminated if liquid latex is stippled over them. For complete elimination of any visible line, several coats of latex may be necessary. If clear medical

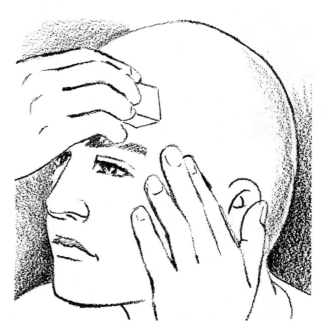

tape has been used, liquid latex can be stippled directly over it. Allow each coat of latex to dry completely before applying another; powder each coat when dry. Drying may be speeded by a portable hair dryer.

2. Paint or spray all dried latex with a coat of plastic sealer or medical spray bandage; allow this to dry, and then powder.

3. After adhering the professional plastic cap to the skin, gently blot the plastic edge with a powder puff that has been dipped in acetone. The entire surrounding edge will completely dissolve onto the skin. *Do not* saturate the plastic edge with acetone, as it will cause large splits in the cap.

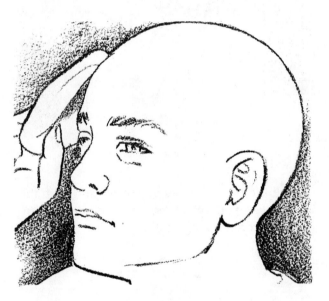

If any edges remain visible, use the aforementioned technique of edge blending with liquid latex and sealer.

Makeup Application:
After sealing the plastic or latex cap, apply a grease base makeup or rubber grease makeup, preferably, to the face and head. To break up the single flat base color, apply highlight and shadow to areas of protrusion and depth, gently blending all the colors. Powder and brush off the excess.

Stipple the cap and face with colored and natural rouges to create a life-like skin texture.

For the effect of a closely shaved scalp, the latex or plastic cap can be stippled in the same manner as a stippled beard.

Character Makeup

SECTION THREE REVIEW

1. Define *(a)* under-base makeup and *(b)* pastel shading.
2. Sketch a character makeup on a chart of the face, incorporating six individual styles from Chapter 17.
3. Because clown makeups are very individual, develop and sketch two original clown makeups.
4. For your picture file, find at least twelve pictures that exemplify the makeup styles of Section Three; at least six of these must be from Chapter 17.
5. Cut a right and left paper pattern for the inner eye tab used to create the Oriental eye.
6. What colors are most compatible with the dark face?
7. On a chart of the face, sketch and design an old-age makeup; indicate areas of highlight and shadow, wrinkles, and lines.
8. Drying and powdering of latex is very important. Why?
9. Discuss two techniques for adhering bald caps to the skin.
10. Where on the face is it not advisable to use wax or putty? Why?
11. Explain three techniques for constructing scars and cuts.
12. Why can't you use most convenient red liquids for blood?

Techniques with Hair

Al Mayton

Preparation and Blending of Crepe Wool and Hair

Chapter 23

Curly Hair Remove the string and separate the wool with the fingers. It can be blended or directly applied.

BLENDING

The beginner can practice with a single shade of hair, but the advanced student must master the art of blending. This is the process by which several colors of hair are mixed together. Blending of hair (crepe wool) will make a hairpiece appear more natural. Choose a color to match the natural hair of the character. This color is called the "base color." Then choose a lighter but compatible shade for edge blending and a darker shade for depth. After selection and preparation, separate the individual shades into lengths approximately 8 inches long.

In preparing crepe wool for beards, moustaches, cap wigs, or chopped-hair beards, one of two techniques may be utilized. Select the proper shade or shades of crepe wool necessary for the project, remembering that several shades can be blended.

Straight Hair Untie the crepe wool; soak it in warm water for half an hour, then hang it up to dry or iron it with a steam iron. This step should be taken early in the procedure so that all moisture can evaporate. After drying, the wool is ready for use.

Techniques with Hair

1. In the palm of the hand, place a length of light wool and a length of the base. Grasp one end firmly and, with the free hand, pull several hairs from each color.

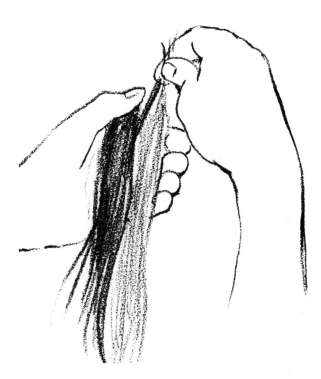

2. Combine them with the original pile in the hand. Repeat the process until both colors have blended into a single shade.

3. Repeat the exact process with the base shade and the darker one.
4. Now you should have five separate shades: Light, light base, base, dark base, and dark. By using all or several of these shades, a natural-appearing hairpiece can be constructed. The chart indicates the approximate area where each shade should be applied. Be creative in the blending and application.

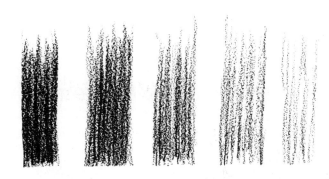

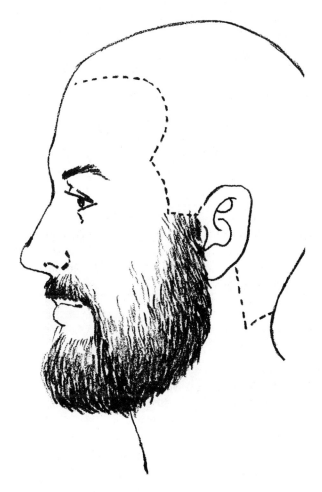

Chopped-hair Beard

Chapter 24

The purpose of the chopped-hair beard is to give the appearance of several days' growth without adding length to the beard. The chopped-hair beard also presents the illusion of natural growth, unlike the stipple beard, which appears flat.

Materials:
> Prepared crepe wool (straight)
> Spirit gum and brush
> Scissors
> Comb
> Acetone, alcohol, and/or Clens makeup remover

Preparation:
After the hair has been straightened, cut lengths ranging from 1/16 to 1/8 inch from about 12 inches of wool. Store the cut wool in a small lidded box.

CREPE WOOL FOR CHOPPED-HAIR BEARD (DARK BROWN)

Application:
1. Remove any makeup from the area where the beard will be applied, because grease does not mix well with spirit gum.
2. If possible, purchase a flat drying gum that does not produce a shine. The wool will have to be applied in sections to keep the gum from drying up. With the brush, paint the prescribed area with gum; stipple it with a piece of old nylon stocking. This helps to remove the shine and makes the gum more adhesive.

3. Remove a ball of wool from the box, pull it in half, and apply it to the gum on the face. Do not press too hard because merely the ends of the hair should adhere, not the whole length of hair. Use each half several times only. Place the remainder back into the box and make another ball, separate it, and apply again to the face. This action is repeated until the entire beard line is covered. If the crepe wool is not adhering to the face, it's because the gum has dried and extra gum must be applied.

4. The wool on the edges should appear sparse. After the applied wool has adhered, comb it through to thin out the edges and heavy spots. Remove or trim any protruding hairs.

Chopped Hair Beard

Constructing and Applying Beards, Moustaches, and Eyebrows

Chapter 25

Materials:
- Crepe wool or hair
- Scissors
- Spirit gum and brush
- Comb
- Acrylic spray (clear)
- Acetone, alcohol, and/or Clens makeup remover

Application:

Hair work should be done in steps so that the artist can always control the flexibility of the hair and the drying time of the gum. It's vital to keep scissors and fingers clean and free of gum by frequently wiping them with Clens makeup remover or acetone. Another point to remember is that the hair should be applied sparingly, because too much hair will cause the beard to flare out.

1. Begin on the neck, directly under the chin in the region of the Adam's apple. Paint this

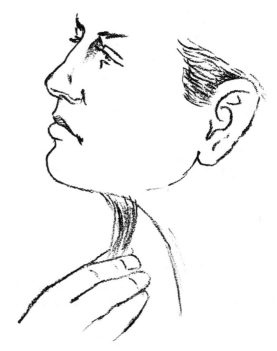

area with gum; make it tacky to remove the shine. This step must be repeated after every application of gum to any facial area. With each application of hair to the face, trim the end applied into a point like a wide tip of an arrow; this kind of trim permits the hair to lie and overlap naturally. Only the ends of the hair should be touched into the gum, and only in the direction along which the arrows on the chart point. (The arrows indicate the natural growth of hair.) Trim the

2. Paint each side under the jaw individually with gum, attach the hair, and trim.

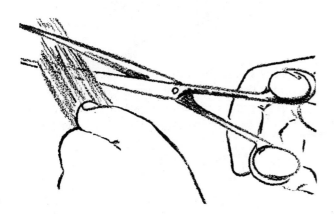

hair with scissors to the desired length. Never trim the hair straight across; always cut it with the angle in which the hair is attached.

3. Paint the chin with gum, etc.
4. Do each side of the face in the same way. When working on sideburns, raise the hair underneath the natural sideburns by pushing upward with the comb and thumb. False

hair can also be attached in front and on top of the natural ones. The outside edge should be very thin. You accomplish this by

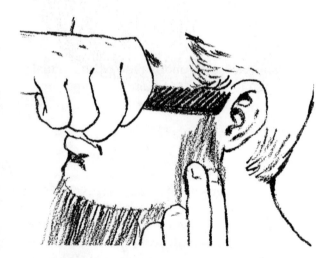

lightly spotting the gum in small areas, fanning the wool, and sparsely adhering the wool to the skin with the points of the scissors.

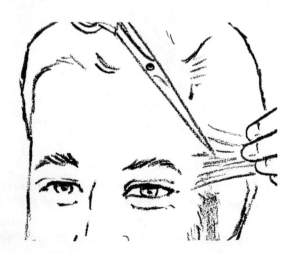

5. Paint the moustache area with gum and apply the hair. Follow the process already discussed to keep the hair thin on the edges.

6. At this point, trim the entire beard and moustache to the exact length desired.

7. Softly press the wool to the face to set the ends. Carefully comb through the hair in the direction of natural growth, being careful not to pull the beard away from the face.

Techniques with Hair

8. If unstraightened hair has been used, it will need little attention except for some combing and a light spray of clear acrylic. If prepared wool has been used, spray lightly over the entire beard and moustache with clear acrylic; then, using the fingers, shape, curl, and swirl the wool into whatever style is required. Finally, snip off any wispy hairs

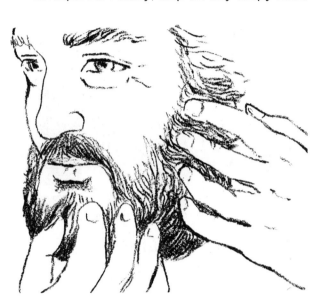

that may protrude. To create a straggly beard, moisten the ends of the fingers with hairstyling gel and work it into the ends of the wool. After the gel has dried, the beard can be sprayed with the clear acrylic spray.

If the beard lies too flat to the face, push it from underneath with the palm of the hand while spraying. This will create a flaring effect.

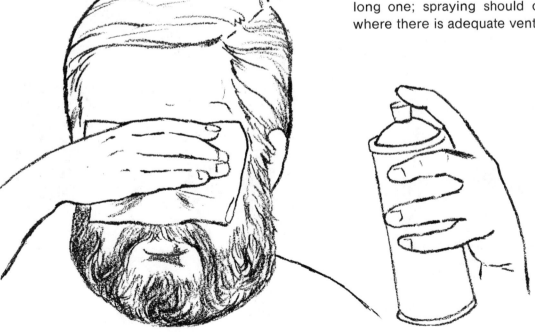

[*Caution:* When using any aerosol sprays, great care should be taken to protect the eyes and nose with a tissue. Do not inhale. Use several short sprays instead of one long one; spraying should only be done where there is adequate ventilation.]

MORE THAN ONCE

If a beard is to be used more than once, give it a second spray of acrylic. This will sufficiently seal the entire piece so that it can be removed from the face and reused. To remove, dip a brush in acetone or Clens makeup remover and apply the solution from the back and inside the piece. Carefully peel the beard away and continue to brush with the remover. When it has

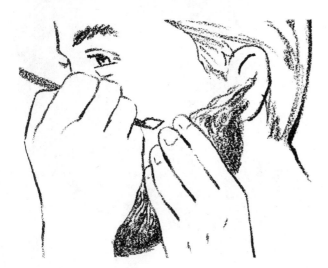

been completely removed from the face, spray inside the piece for added strength. Whenever spraying, hold the spray can at least 12 to 18 inches away from the hair pieces. With care, this type of beard will last through several performances and is considered a satisfactory kind of ready-made beard.

HOW TO APPLY A READY-MADE BEARD

1. There must be no grease base on skin where the spirit gum is applied. The skin should be dry, clean, and powdered.
2. Hold the beard in place on the face and mark the outside edges with a light eyebrow pencil.

3. Remove beard and paint all the exposed facial area inside the outlines with spirit gum.

Techniques with Hair

4. Make the gum tacky with the fingers, subsequently cleaning fingers.

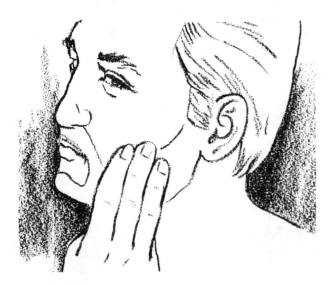

5. After you replace the beard and press it into the gum, some edges may need touching up.

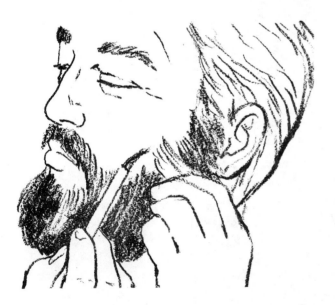

6. Following the second performance the beard should be removed as carefully as the first time and set aside for later use.

EYEBROWS

Eyebrows are an important adjunct to a finished character makeup. Character styles can be drawn on with eyebrow pencils, colored with sprays, or more fully developed with overlying crepe wool.

Application:
1. Crepe wool can be used in the curly state if it is separated from the original braid.

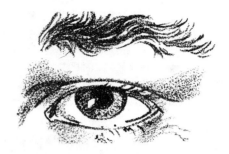

2. It can be attached after the straightening process at an upward or downward angle.

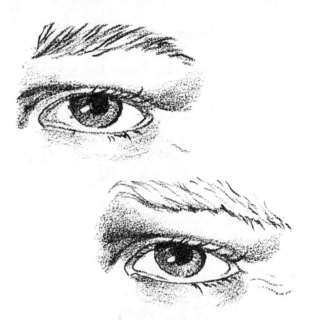

3. A straightened piece can be curled by being wrapped around a ½- or 1-inch wooden dowel and sprayed with clear acrylic. Allow it to dry, and remove from the dowel; cut off the length of curl desired and adhere it to the section of natural brow where the character is to be emphasized. The ends may be separated and trimmed if necessary.

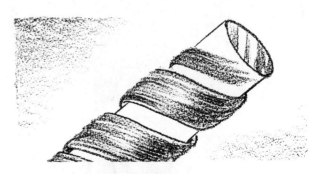

Constructing and Applying Beards

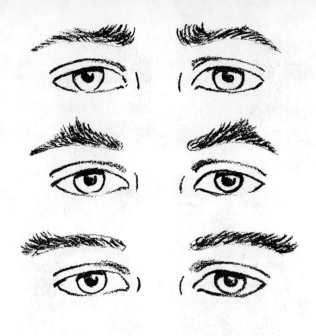

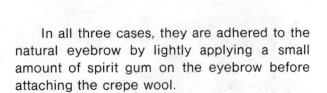

In all three cases, they are adhered to the natural eyebrow by lightly applying a small amount of spirit gum on the eyebrow before attaching the crepe wool.

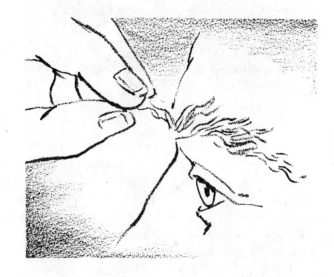

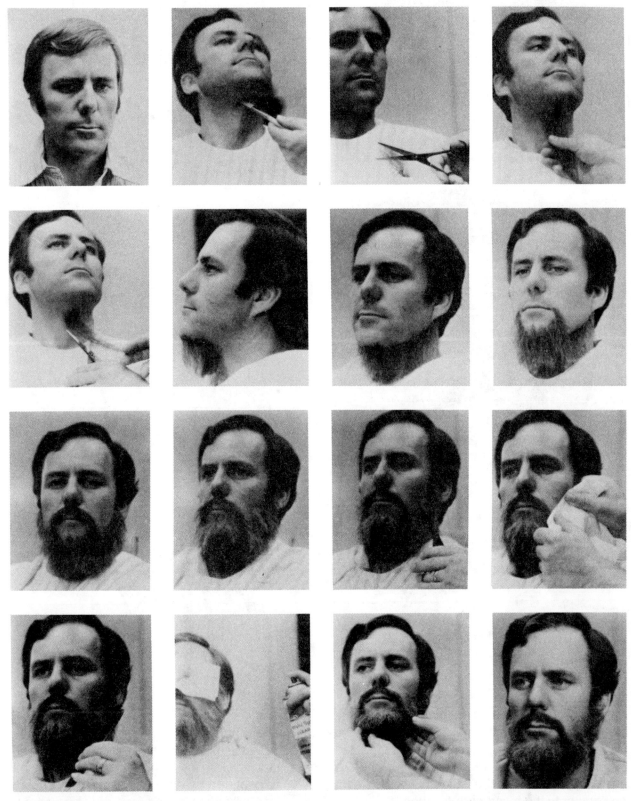

CONSTRUCTING A BEARD   To begin constructing a crepe wool beard, the wool must be straightened and blended, and the necessary tools laid out.   Start on the neck directly under the chin. The area is painted with spirit gum and allowed to become tacky. A length of wool is then trimmed at an angle and touched onto the tacky gum. Each time a new length of crepe wool is adhered, it is trimmed off in the direction in which it was touched.

There is a continuous overlapping of wool while the entire beard is being constructed. The wool used for the edges should be a light shade and spread very sparsely. When all the wool has been adhered, the entire beard is trimmed to the exact length desired.

With the hands the wool is pressed firmly to the face, setting the adhered ends. Being careful not to pull the beard away from the face, draw a comb through carefully, removing loose hairs and thick areas.

For a lasting finish the beard is sprayed with a clear acrylic spray, swirled, curled, and shaped into its final style. The eyes and nose must always be protected when using any kind of spray.

Hair Lace Foundations

Chapter 26

Application and Care:

An enormous amount of training and practice are needed to master the art of tying hair lace pieces; the technique, therefore, is not included in this volume. Since ready-made lace pieces are easily obtained, the student should learn how to apply them and care for them.

ADHERING

Materials:

Spirit gum

Nylon stocking

Application:

1. The entire area where the lace will lie against the skin should be thoroughly cleaned with a skin freshener to remove oil.
2. Except for the place where the exposed lace edge lies on the face, the face should be painted with gum before the lace piece is applied. Tack up the gum with the finger and wipe fingers clean.
3. Center the lace piece and press it into place.

Techniques with Hair

5. Take a nylon stocking and press the lace into the face, always rotating the nylon to a clean area. By this technique, the lace is made invisible against the skin.

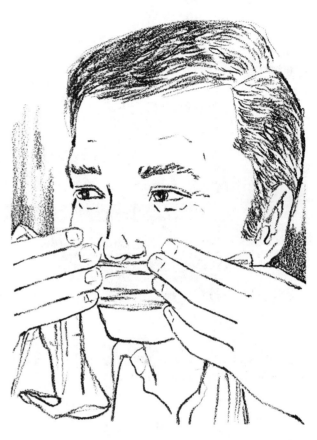

4. Run a small brush, dipped in gum, under the lace edge.

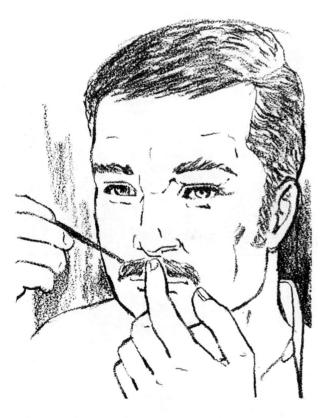

6. Makeup should never be applied over hair lace, but blended directly up to it.

CARE AND CLEANING

Materials:
    Acetone
    Small china bowl
    Stiff bristle brush
    Paper towel

Method:
1. Pour a small amount of acetone into a bowl and immerse the lace in it.

2. Remove the piece and lay it, lace side down, on the paper towel.

4. Allow the piece to air dry briefly; then pin it to a wig block so that it will retain its shape and be ready for use at the next performance.

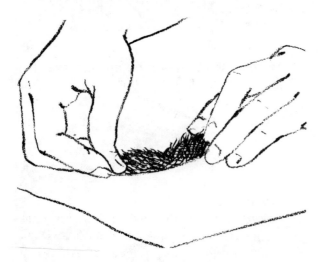

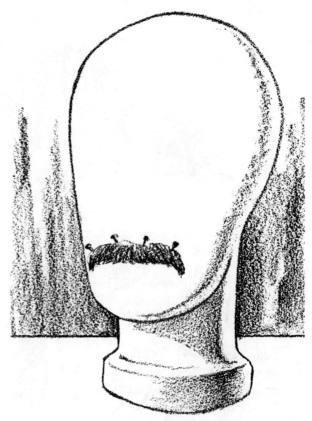

3. Dip the stiff brush into the acetone and lightly tap the piece with the bristles of the brush. The old gum will come off on the paper.

Latex Foundations

Chapter 27

If a beard is to be worn for any length of time, it's advisable to construct it on a latex foundation or purchase a lace one. Latex foundations can be constructed either on the performer's face or on a plaster life mask.

Materials:

Liquid latex
Latex color (flesh tone)
Brush—½-inch, disposable
Gauze bandage—1-inch
Scissors
Rubber or neoprene cement or spirit gum with sealer, 2:1
Portable hair dryer

Construction:

1. Color the liquid latex with a flesh-tone pigment. Use only a small amount because the pigments are highly concentrated. Check the color after each addition because the latex will dry much darker than its color in the liquid state.
2. Paint one coat of latex on the performer's face or on the life mask. Paint it at least ¼ inch smaller than the size desired. Allow this to dry and powder it. This is to allow sufficient margin for a thin layer of hair along the edge to hide the latex foundation.

4. Adhesive must be applied in sections to the latex foundation in the same manner as described earlier. Apply adhesive to the foundation and allow it to stand until tacky.

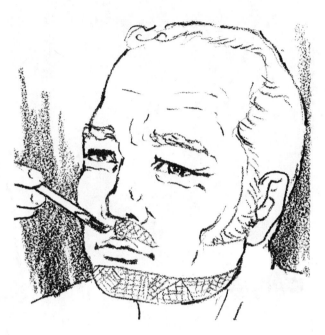

3. Cut the 1-inch gauze bandage into small triangles. With the brush, rubberize a second coat of latex and gauze onto the first one, slightly overlapping the triangles as they are applied. Dry the latex and bandage by blowing warm air on it from a portable hair dryer. Apply a third coat of latex over all, dry, and powder.

5. Tap the prepared hair into the adhesive with the tips of the scissors. Be sure to keep the scissors clean. Always make sure the ends of hair to be set into the adhesive are even, because wild hairs can cause problems.

Techniques with Hair

6. Trim off the excess hair in the direction of natural growth, slightly longer than the final desired shape.

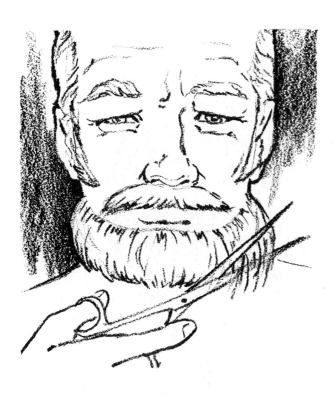

7. Lightly spray with clear acrylic and shape with the fingers. Hold the spray at least 12 inches away.

8. With a pointed wood modeling tool, lift a back corner of the latex foundation, grasp with the fingers, and gently pull away from the face.

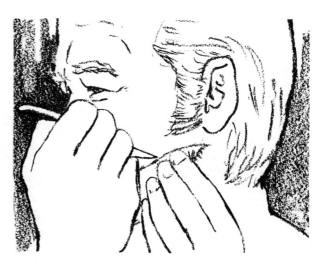

9. Powder the inside and allow to air dry.
10. Latex foundations are best applied with liquid latex since old coats can easily be removed. Spirit gum can also be used, but later it's much more difficult to remove.
11. Last, add a small line of new hair over the edge to hide the latex border.

Wigs

Chapter 28

If a natural-appearing wig is needed, it's best to comparison shop at various local beauty supply sources and discount wig centers to find the best buy.

Purchasing:
1. Select proper color.
2. Texture of hair—coarse hair is harder to curl then the more manageable fine hair.
3. Check for comfortable fit.
4. Price—up to $25.
5. Avoid synthetics unless they are permanently styled or the hair is to be worn straight or in buns; many synthetics do not hold their styling during rugged performances.

6. If the wig is for a period style, necessary trimming should be done by a professional hair stylist.
7. Avoid heavy hair sprays which are difficult to remove from the wig. A light spray, with some shine, is recommended because wigs quickly lose luster characteristic of natural hair.
8. Purchase a styrofoam wig block that will fit the wig.

Setting:
1. Secure the wig to the block with five 3-inch pins—one on each temple, one on the top front edge, and one on each side of the neck.

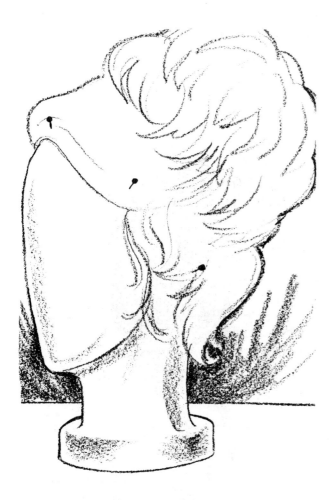

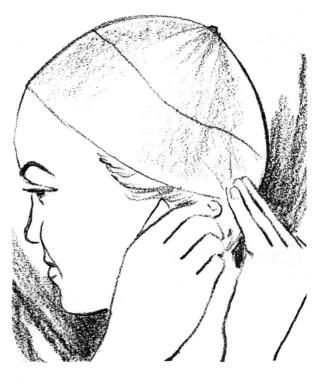

2. Place the wig on the head and anchor with large hair pins.
3. Anchor the wig in the front, in the back, and on each side for security.

2. Do thorough research to discover the exact style needed.
3. The rollers should be directed in the order in which the hair will be combed out when dry. Pin curls are recommended for the sides so that the hair will cling to the face.
4. After the rollers have been placed, lightly spray the hair with water or nondulling setting lotion.
5. Place a hair net over the wig and dry thoroughly on the block.
6. Remove the rollers and pins, and brush wig thoroughly.
7. Lightly back brush the hair for an airy appearance.
8. With a styling comb, arrange hair in the predetermined fashion.
9. Spray with the water-soluble hair spray.
10. Remove the anchor pins.

Applying:
1. Wrap the performer's hair in a stocking cap, making certain that all the hair is pulled underneath and evenly distributed.

4. Rearrange the hair to compliment the performer's face.

Removal:
Carefully remove the hair pins; replace the wig on the block with the five anchor pins.

Cleaning:
Wig cleaners are readily available at beauty supply shops. Follow the manufacturer's directions carefully.

Latex Cap Wig

For inexpensive productions, or instances when a special style of wig is needed, you can easily construct a wig on a latex foundation. If special colors of hair are needed, white crepe wool can be dyed almost any shade with temporary vegetable rinses. When preparing to papier-mâché a styrofoam head block for latex cap wigs, exact head sizes can be duplicated if the natural head size is measured as follows, carrying out steps 1 to 5. Then reconstruct with papier-mâché until the desired shape has been duplicated.

Note: To ensure a snug fit for bald caps, the styrofoam block must be smaller than normal head size.

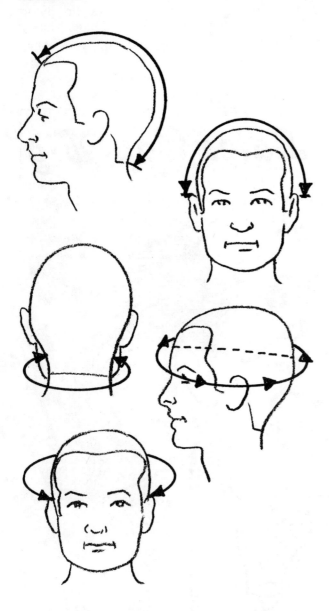

Materials:
   Rubber or neoprene cement and brush
   Prepared crepe wool
   Scissors
   Metal comb
   Wig block
   Latex bald cap

Construction:
   1. Place the latex cap on a wig block.

2. Lay out the prepared and blended crepe wool.

3. Beginning at the nape of the neck, attach the hair according to the directional chart.

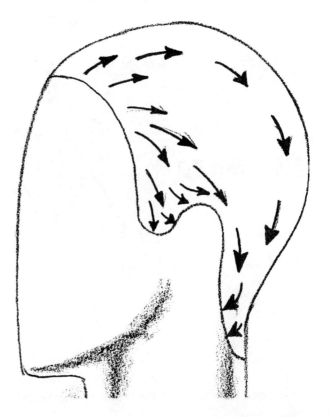

Techniques with Hair

Work on only a small area at a time, because the adhesive dries quickly. Be sure the ends of the crepe wool are well adhered to the glue; press them down with the back of the comb and allow to dry.

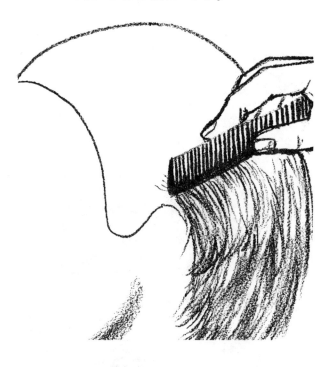

4. Trim off the desired length of hair at the angle of natural growth, not straight across.

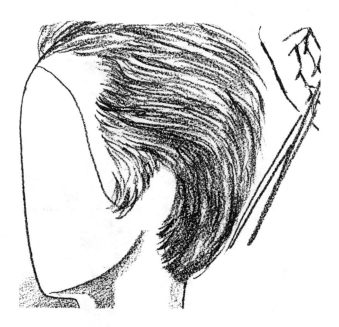

5. When the entire cap has been covered with hair, gently comb through it to remove excess hair. Start at the nape of the neck;

with one hand firmly hold the roots of the hair, and with the other hand comb through gently. Always hold the comb with the teeth pointing toward the roots, and lightly drag through. Never pull down.

6. Generally, the adhesive is strong enough so that the crepe wool hair can be styled like other wigs. It may be gently rolled, combed out, styled, and sprayed. After being applied to the head, it must be styled to cover all exposed edges of the cap. If a partially bald effect is desired, then the latex edge in front can be treated as a bald area. Styling gels, rather than oil or greases, should be used, since this type of wig is difficult to clean. If a permanent style is wanted, spray the entire completed piece with a mist of clear acrylic spray. Exposed latex on the frontal sections of the partial pieces can be made up with highlights, shadows, stippling, and painted wrinkles.

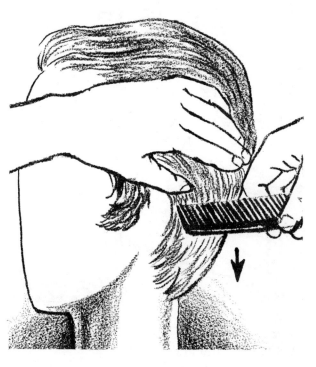

NATURAL HAIRLINE EFFECT

To create a more natural hairline effect, you can insert individual strands of hair through a latex cap and secure them from the inside. An entire wig may be constructed this way. To save time you can use this technique around the edges only.

Material:
- Latex cap
- Fine sewing needle, nippers
- Crepe wool or hair
- Rubber adhesive

Construction:

1. Snip off one-half of the eye of a fine sewing needle.

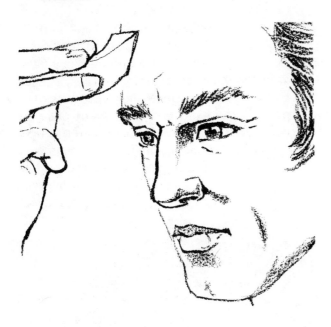

2. Lay a few hairs over the spot where hair is going to be inserted.

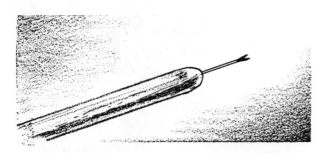

3. Place the fork of the pin over the hair and force it through the latex surface.

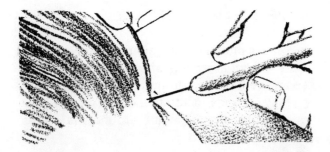

4. Pull the hair through far enough to tie a small knot on the inside end.

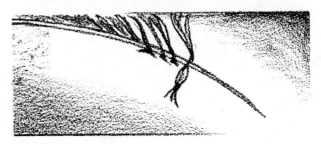

5. After inserting and tying all the hair needed, paint the inside knots with the rubber adhesive. Always paint in the direction opposite to that in which the hair will lie; this allows for easier styling.

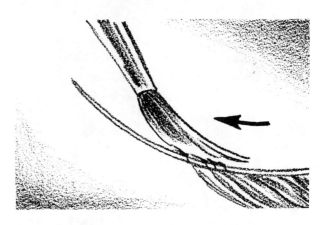

6. After the inside adhesive has dried, powder it. The wig is now ready to be placed on a block for an easy combout and styling.

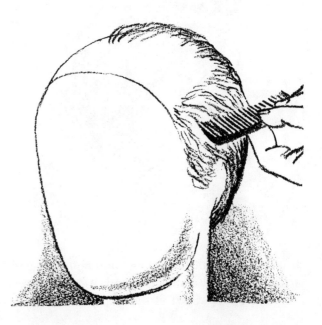

Techniques with Hair

Hair Coloring

Chapter 30

The quickest and fastest procedure for changing the color of an actor's hair is to use colored hair sprays or temporary vegetable rinses. When applying the color, remember to protect the face and clothing. Follow the manufacturer's directions precisely.

Application of sprays:

1. It's best to spray the hair in sections. Lightly part the hair, spray, and comb. Continue doing this until all the hair is colored.
2. There is no problem coloring light hair, but darker hair needs extra treatment. An undercoat of spray is required to lighten darker hair. For example, before being sprayed white, dark hair must first be sprayed with a yellowish tone such as blond or beige. To be sprayed a color such as pink or green, dark hair must also be sprayed first with white.

3. Other products used for coloring hair, especially for the graying of hair, are distributed by the theatrical cosmetic suppliers. These specially prepared liquids or water-soluble cake makeups (such as white cake makeup) are stroked into the hair with a dye brush or toothbrush.

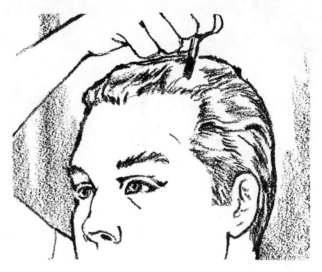

4. If streaks are desired, spray the color or pour the liquid color into an open container, or moisten the cake makeup; then, with a dye brush or old toothbrush, stroke it onto the individual hairs.

6. I would like to caution the actor against using any products on the hair which have not been manufactured by a cosmetic company and which cannot be easily removed by a good shampooing.

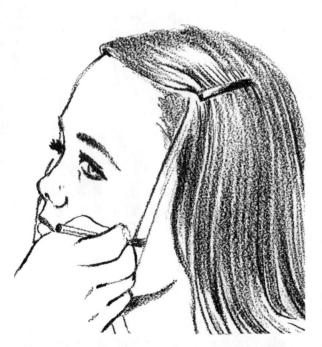

5. If the entire head of hair has been coated with a single color, it may appear dull. Highlights or shadows can be added to the colored hair by spraying or brushing areas with a complimentary shade.

Techniques with Hair

SECTION FOUR REVIEW

1. Define the phrase "blending of hair or crepe wool." What is the purpose of blending?
2. Define the principal difference between a stippled beard and a chopped-hair beard.
3. With reference to attaching prepared hair or wool to the face, evaluate the following statements and elaborate on the correct answers:
   a. Begin by painting the entire face with spirit gum.
   b. Apply the hair flat to the face for more security.
   c. Trim the hair straight across.
   d. Set and style hair goods with clear acrylic spray.
   e. Spirit gum adheres best over a makeup base.
4. Name the two different materials from which foundations for lasting hair pieces can be made.
5. Spirit gum should be removed from hair lace with (select one): Clens makeup remover, soap and water, acetone, cleansing cream.
6. For your picture file, collect at least eight examples representing natural growth and direction of beards, wigs, moustaches, and eyebrows.
7. With reference to hair coloring:
   a. What is the purpose of an undercoat of colored spray?
   b. How are colored streaks added?
8. List four similarities between constructing a latex beard foundation and a cap wig.

Prosthetics

Al Mayton

Introduction to Prosthetics

Chapter 31

Of all the techniques that have been described up to this point, none is more important than the creation of theatrical prosthetics. This section deals with the casting of a life mask impression, the construction of a theatrical prosthetic, and the special makeup involved.

Knowledge of this procedure is extremely beneficial because of the unlimited possibilities it permits for both makeup artist and performer. The wearing of a prosthetic builds up a feeling of inner security in an actor as he portrays a role.

With the prosthetic technique, individual pieces or full masks can be constructed to adhere directly to the face. For example, individual sections of bags, jowls, and folds can be developed to represent old age or a more complex type of Oriental eye. These individual prosthetics may also be used to create monsters, life-size animals, and numerous other characters.

No matter how courageous a person is, he experiences some apprehension when a cast of his face is taken. Although the technique is safe, the subject's feelings and attitude must be considered. The makeup artist should have a confident, quiet approach when doing a facial cast.

Simple Prosthetics

Chapter 32

There are several different techniques for developing facial prosthetics. Some of the faster and simpler forms are wax, papier-mâché, and slip casting.

WAX

Wax is easily shaped for the face, but it won't always appear the same for every performance. (Refer to an earlier chapter covering the process of wax application.) Wax is always applied the same way, no matter what form or shape.

PAPIER-MÂCHÉ

This is an old technique mainly used for creating masks, but facial appliances can also be constructed with it. Basic materials for it may be purchased in local art stores, or you may follow the formula for covering the wig block in Chapter 23.

1. For best results, a life impression should be taken of the actor who will be wearing the piece.

2. When the plaster mask has dried, paint it with castor oil to leave a thin sticky surface.

3. Apply small pieces of oil clay or wet clay to the plaster face and model it into the desired shape.

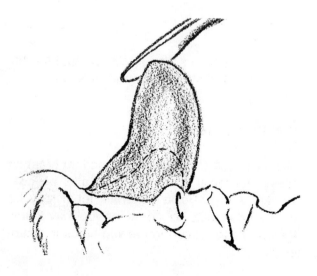

4. When the shape is complete, cover it with at least three layers of papier-mâché, gently smoothing down the layers to conform with the clay modeling.

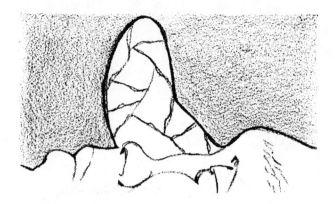

5. Allow this to dry. With fine sandpaper, smooth off any rough edges and coat it with shellac. Several applications of shellac may be necessary.

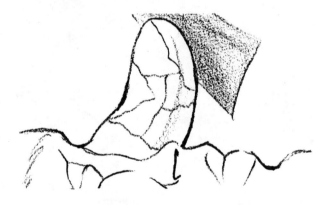

6. Paint the papier-mâché with any durable, flexible variety of paint. Rubber-base paints are excellent, since they do not chip or crack.

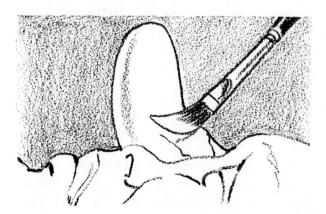

Prosthetics

7. Remove the papier-mâché model from the plaster cast and clean out the clay. Wet clay is removed with water, and oil is removed with alcohol.

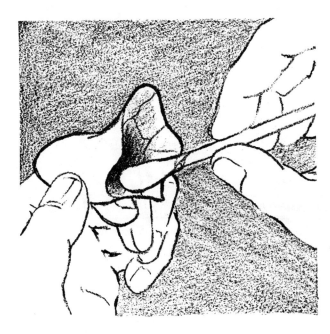

SLIP CASTING

1. Again, a cast of the performer is recommended; after the cast has dried sufficiently, paint it with shellac.

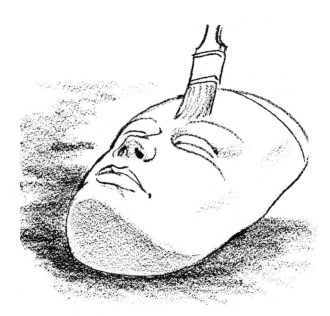

2. On the sealed cast, model the piece needed with oil or wet clay.

3. Clean any excess clay that has rubbed onto the model with the proper solvent (water or alcohol).

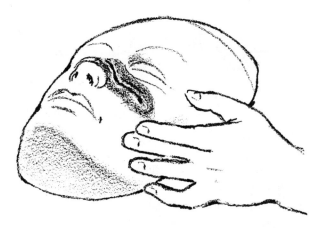

4. Rub a thin coat of Vaseline petroleum jelly over the remainder of the exposed plaster.
5. Cover the modeling with a layer of casting plaster at least 1 inch thick. This generates heat as it hardens, but can be removed when cool.

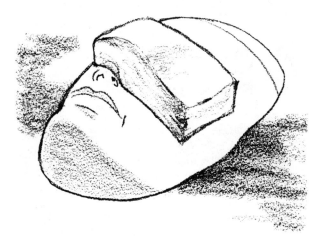

6. Separate the plaster mold from the plaster face, and clean off the clay from both sides. To avoid scratching models, always use a wooden tool for removing clay.

7. Allow the mold to dry overnight in a warm place.

8. Pouring latex: Support the mold so that it opens from the top. Fill it with slip-casting latex and let it stand for fifteen to thirty minutes, depending on the thickness desired. Pour off the excess and allow to drain for half an hour.

9. Dry the latex in a warm place. To speed drying, direct the warm air from a portable hair dryer into the mold.

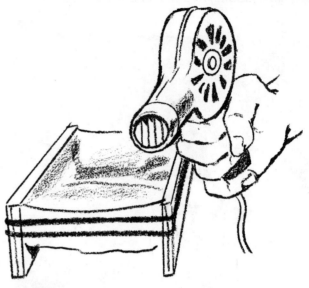

10. When the latex is no longer wet to the touch, remove it from the mold and allow the surface to cure in open air.

11. When dry, the latex can be prepainted with latex paint matching the makeup.

The piece is now ready to be secured to the face with spirit gum or two-way tape. If not prepainted, it can then be made up with rubber grease makeup.

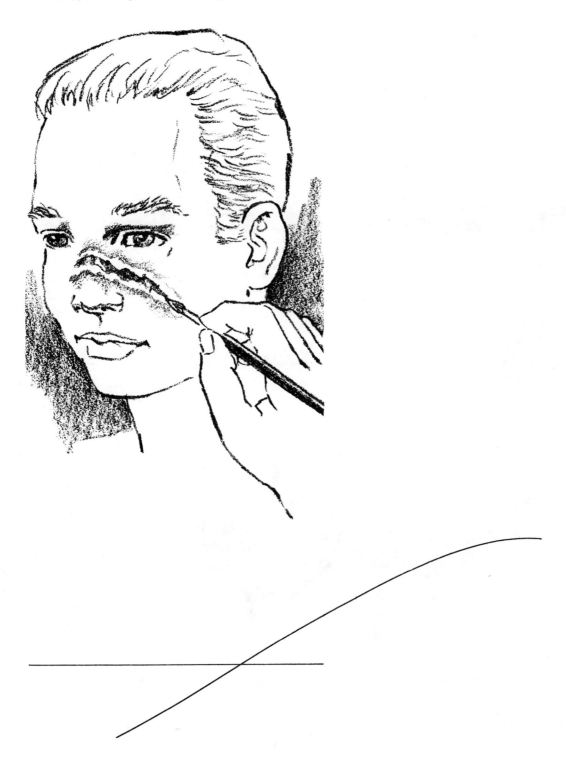

Casting the Face

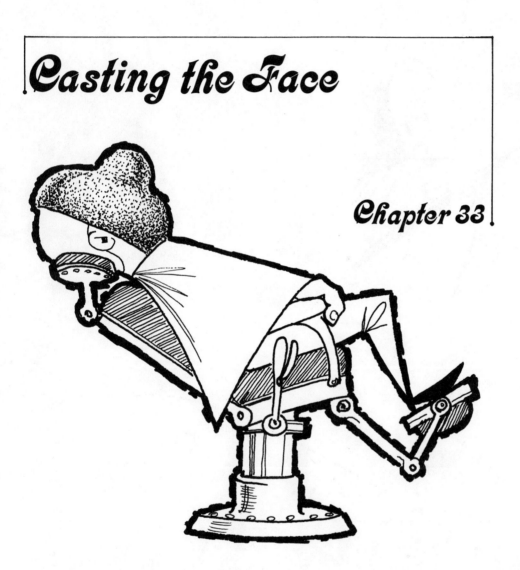

Chapter 33

PREPARATION OF THE SUBJECT

Materials:

Plastic hair cloth or disposable towel
Vaseline petroleum jelly
Rubber bald cap or bathing cap

A high chair with back
Medical clear tape

Method:

1. The subject should sit in an elevated chair so that the makeup artist will not need to

Prosthetics

bend over. Place the plastic hair cloth or towel around the subject's neck and secure it tightly.

2. Fit the rubber cap over the head to cover the hair. If necessary, the cap can be secured with spirit gum under the edge, or pieces of clear tape can be pressed over the outside edge.

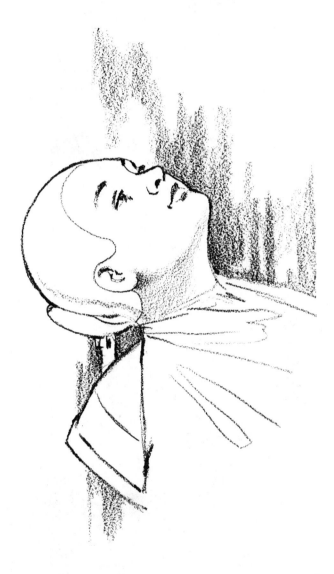

3. Moustaches or beards should be covered with tape because, if they remain exposed and become impregnated, the impression material may tear when removed. All exposed hair, such as eyebrows, eyelashes, or sideburns, should be lightly smeared with petroleum jelly for easier release. It is important *not* to rub petroleum jelly over the entire face because it makes the plaster surface become powdery.

PREPARATION OF MATERIALS

Duplicating compounds (warm molding materials) and alginate (cold molding material) are used for facial impressions. The materials can be purchased at specific theatrical makeup sources, local art and craft stores, or local dental suppliers. Follow any general instructions given by individual manufacturers.

PREPARATION OF MOULAGE

Materials:
    Moulage
    Double boiler
    Spoon
    Hot plate
    Water

Method:
1. Before the subject is prepared, the moulage should be cooked for forty-five minutes to one hour to become free of lumps and reach a creamy consistency.
2. Fill the bottom half of a kitchen double boiler with water and the top half with the moulage.
3. Place the double boiler on a hot plate or stove to cook the moulage; stir occasionally with a spoon to break up any lumps.
4. If the material is too thick and not brushable, slowly add small amounts of water to thin the mixture.
5. When the moulage has reached a creamy consistency, cool by placing the upper half of the double boiler into cold water. Stir vigorously.

6. Test the material by placing a drop on the skin. When it is tolerable, but still hot, it is ready for application.

APPLICATION OF MOULAGE

Materials:
 Brush—1-inch utility
 Brush—small, round water color no. 3

Method:
 1. The face should be held at a slight angle backward, with the chin tilted up, the eyes closed, and the back of the head supported.
 2. Using the 1-inch brush, apply the material.

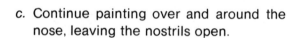

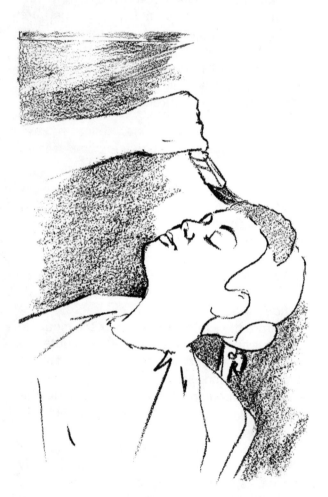

c. Continue painting over and around the nose, leaving the nostrils open.

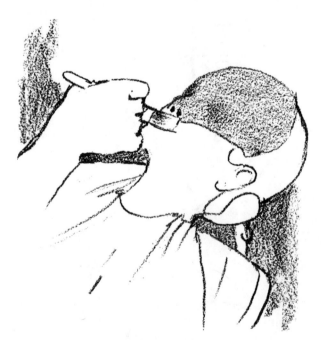

 a. Start at the top of the head about halfway back.
 b. Paint down the forehead and over the eyes, being careful not to trap any air in the corner of the eyes.

 d. Paint back to the front of the ears but do not cover. If needed, ear casts should be taken separately; a small piece of cotton must be placed in ears before they are covered.

Prosthetics

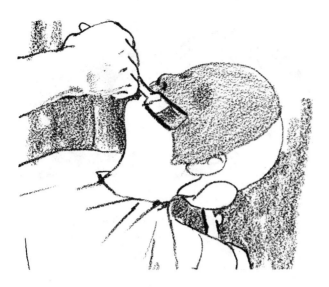

e. Continue down the face over the mouth, around the jaw, and down the neck to the collarbone.

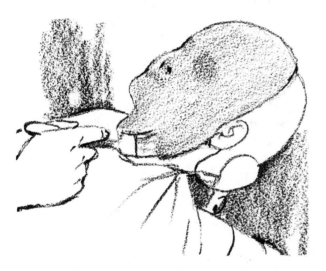

f. With the small brush, paint around and slightly up into the nostrils.

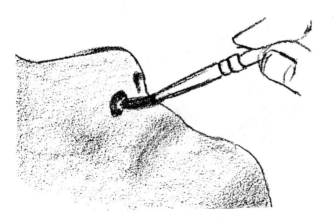

g. Be sure that the entire coat is at least ¼ inch thick, otherwise thin areas will quickly shrink and tear.

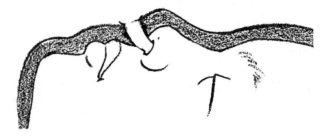

3. The painting should be accomplished as rapidly and smoothly as possible. When casting partial areas of the face, such as the nose, be sure to include an adequate border. If high peaks or globs of material begin to occur, it means the material has begun to solidify; more heated material can be applied, however, because material bonds to itself.

4. Since moulage has such excellent release attributes, the double boiler and the brushes can be easily cleaned by being soaked in hot water and wiped clean.

PREPARATION OF ALGINATE

Materials (for one full face):
    Large mixing bowl
    Cool water, 70°F, 40 ounces or 4 to 5 cups
    Alginate (12 ounces or 1½ cups)
    Large mixing spoon

Smaller amounts of alginate and water may be used for impressions of smaller areas of the face.

Method:
1. Pour the alginate into a clean, dry mixing bowl and add the premeasured water. The temperature of the water should be approximately 70°F; colder water will slow down the setting time of the alginate, whereas warmer water will speed it up. The approximate proportion is three to four parts water and one part alginate.

2. Quickly mix the two ingredients together for one minute to form a smooth creamy mixture. Do not overmix, because this material sets in just a few minutes.

APPLICATION OF ALGINATE

1. When applying alginate to the face, have an assistant help you because the material has a tendency to flow down. With the hands, apply the material to the face, starting at the forehead. Continually gather up the excess alginate and apply until it hardens. The assistant should carefully watch the subject's nostrils to keep the breathing passages open. The passages can be kept open with a wooden modeling tool.

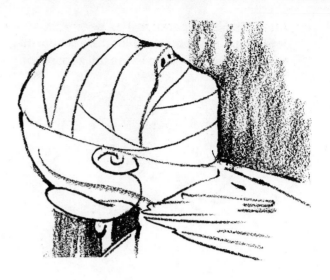

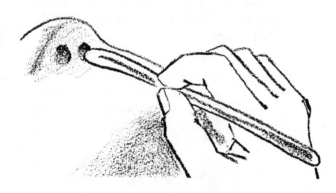

2. When the alginate begins to harden, it becomes lumpy. From the first sign of lumpiness, the material will set within seconds.

Additional Notes:
1. Be careful to mix enough alginate for the entire job because additional material, added later, will not bond to a coat that has already hardened. Make a test with 1 ounce of alginate before attempting larger mixes.
2. Pour the plaster positive immediately, because the alginate slowly shrinks when exposed to the air.
3. Several plaster copies can be made from a single alginate impression if the first copy can be removed without damage to the foundation.
4. A piece of wire coathanger, bent and imbedded into the wet plaster, can provide an implement for separating the two facial impressions.

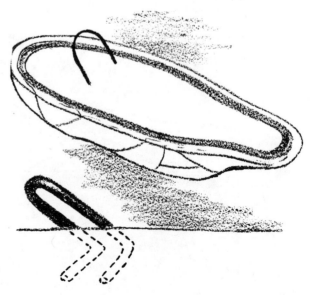

3. When the alginate has solidified, back it with plaster bandage for support.

5. After a small separation has been made, a few drops of water sprinkled between the two casts will also help in the full separation.

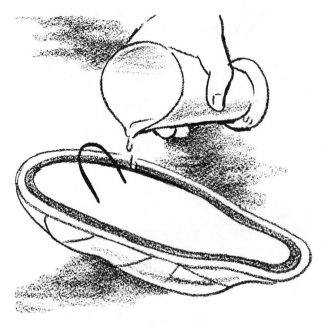

PLASTER BANDAGE SUPPORT

Materials:

    A roll of 2-inch plaster bandage (fast-setting) or plaster of paris

    Scissors

    Plastic bowl filled with water at room temperature

    Small wood modeling tool

Method:

1. Follow the steps for mixing loose plaster, or cut the plaster bandage into 4- and 6-inch strips; one 6-inch strip should be cut into small half-inch triangles.

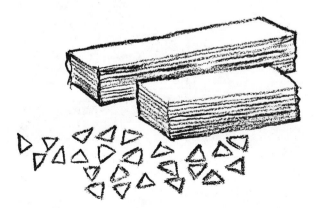

2. Dip the plaster bandage, one strip at a time, into the water and apply the bandage over the impression material. Continue doing this until the entire face has been coated at least three times; be certain to overlap the bandage to add extra strength to the plaster support.

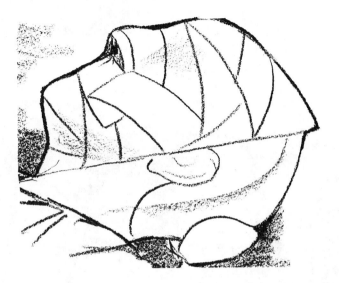

3. Dip the triangles, one at a time, into the water and apply them around and inside the nostril, keeping them on the moulage and not on the skin. With the small modeling tool, press the corners of the plaster triangles down around and inside the nose.

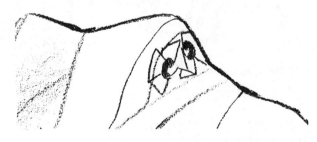

4. Drying time of the plaster bandage varies with the temperature of the water and the humidity in the air. Refer to the label for drying instructions; I have discovered, however, that twenty to thirty minutes is usually adequate drying time.

5. Plaster has a natural tendency to generate heat when hardening, but do not let the warmth disturb you. The plaster has not

been actually set until the surface has cooled.

REMOVAL OF IMPRESSION MATERIAL AND PLASTER SUPPORT

1. Have subject sit straight in the chair.
2. Tilt subject's head forward.
3. Gently release the attached material from around the edges of the face.
4. Pull forward and down.

POURING THE POSITIVE CAST OR LIFE MASK

Materials:
Wet clay
Clear acrylic spray
Plastic bowl (about 5 inches deep by 12 inches across)
Hydrocal Plaster (a hard-setting plaster) or dental stone
Kitchen knife, blunt edge
Paper towels

Utility brush—1-inch
Vaseline petroleum jelly

Construction:
1. After removing the combined support and impression material from the face, spray with acrylic, and fill the nostril holes from the outside with wet clay to prevent leakage.

2. Put a thin coat of petroleum jelly over any exposed plaster bandage on the inside of the mold.

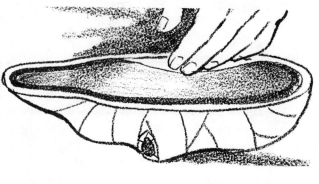

3. To measure the water for the plaster, fill the head three-quarters full and pour the water into the plastic bowl.

Prosthetics

4. Towel dry the excess water that is on the impression.

5. *Without putting your hand in the water,* begin slowly shaking the plaster into the bowl until the plaster rises to a level just above the water line.

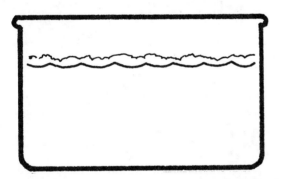

6. Let mixture stand for about five minutes or until all the dry plaster has been absorbed.
7. Support the mold on both sides, and under the nose, with clay so that it won't fall over.

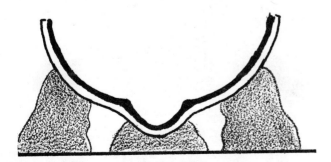

8. Dip your hands into the bowl and stir slowly, breaking up any lumps you discover. Continue doing this until a cream-like mixture is reached. Plaster which has not been mixed thickly enough may bring about powdering on the surface of the mold when dry.

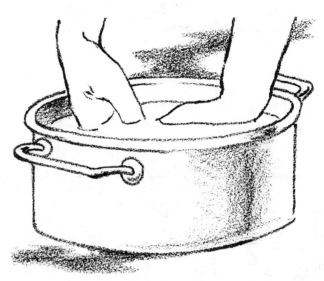

9. With the 1-inch brush, paint on the first plaster coat thoroughly to build up a sturdy surface for the dry positive mold. Immediately wash out the brush and the hands.

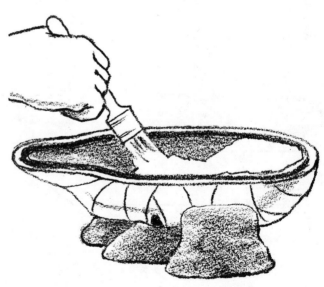

10. Partially fill the mold with plaster and carefully vibrate it to release any trapped air bubbles. Do not fill the negative mold full of plaster because the pressure will force the mold out of shape.

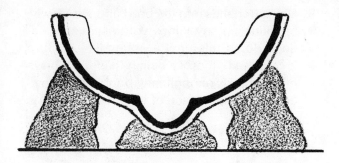

12. Let the mold stand until the plaster has cooled; then try to remove the plaster bandage in one piece, or peel it off. Unused moulage can be saved for further work, but excess alginate must be discarded.

13. When the plaster face is dry, wash it to remove any residue. Stiff brushes and wooden tools can also be used to clean the completed face.

11. With the knife, smooth the plaster up along the sides of the impression material until the plaster is set. The finished plaster cast should be no thicker than 1 to 1½ inches.

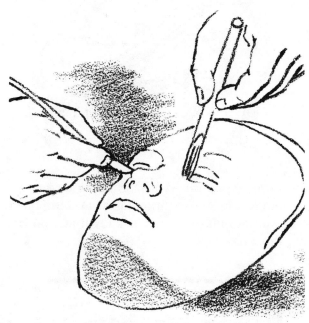

Mounting the Positive Cast

Materials:

    A 5-foot length of 1- by 1-inch pine lumber
    Saw, nails, hammer, ruler
    Wet clay
    Vaseline petroleum jelly
    Hydrocal Plaster (a hard-setting plaster)
    Can of clear acrylic spray
    Kitchen knife, with a blunt edge

Construction:

1. Construct a wooden frame that will permit at least a 3-inch margin around the plaster life mask. For example, if the head is 8 by 4 inches, the inside measurements would be 14 by 10 inches.

Chapter 34

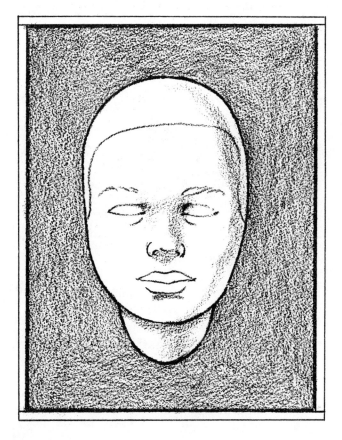

2. Paint the frame with shellac or spray it with acrylic spray; let the material dry.

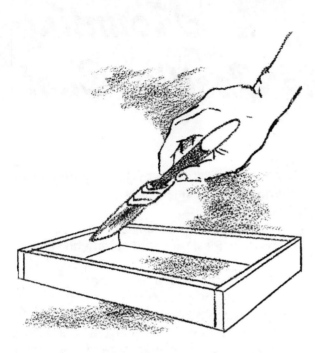

3. Lay the frame on a nonporous surface, such as plastic, Formica laminated plastic, or glass; seal the outside bottom edge with wet clay to prevent the wet plaster from running out underneath.

5. Mix the plaster as outlined in Chapter 33, but use 2 quarts of water in the plastic bowl.
6. Soak the life mask in water to keep it from absorbing moisture from the wet plaster when immersed.
7. Pour the frame three-fourths full of wet plaster and let stand until it has the consistency of thick pudding. If foam rubber is to be used, substitute step 12 (below) for step 7.

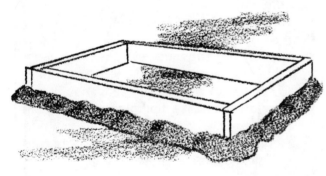

4. Seal the inside of the frame, its top, and the nonporous bottom with a thin coat of prepared petroleum jelly (a mixture of kerosene and Vaseline petroleum jelly made as follows: Melt several heaping tablespoons of Vaseline over low heat. Remove Vaseline from the heat and stir in, slowly, sufficient kerosene to hold the cooled mixture in a liquid state; the ratio is three parts kerosene to one part Vaseline.)

8. Remove the plaster life mask from the water in which it was soaking. Dry off excess water and place it into the wet plaster, making certain that a 3-inch margin surrounds the head. Fill the frame to the top with remaining plaster. Also, do not tilt the head to either side but place it in a straight, level position.

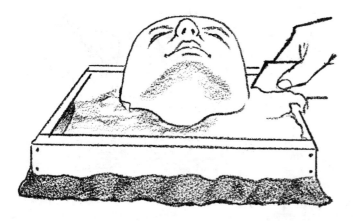

9. When the plaster is very heavy and creamy, fill in any holes that may remain at the top of the head or the neck; with the knife scrape off any plaster that is higher than the frame. The marginal area that surrounds the head should be flat and level with the top of the frame. Let the mask stand until dry to the touch.

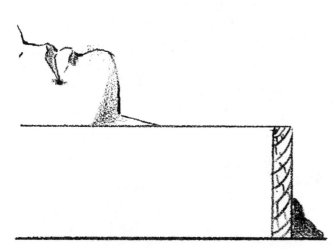

10. Before the plaster has completely cooled, carve out a small sloping hole on each corner approximately 1 inch in from the out-

side edge. Use the blunt edge of the knife to do this. These holes will be used for later alignment of the two halves.

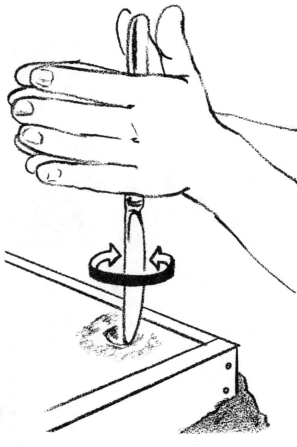

11. When the plaster has cooled, knock away the wooden frame.
12. For added strength, especially if foam rubber is to be used, fill the frame one-fourth full of wet plaster, immerse hemp fiber or thread-like fiberglass into it, then fill the frame three-fourths full with the remaining wet plaster. Then continue process as directed in step 8.

Modeling with Clay

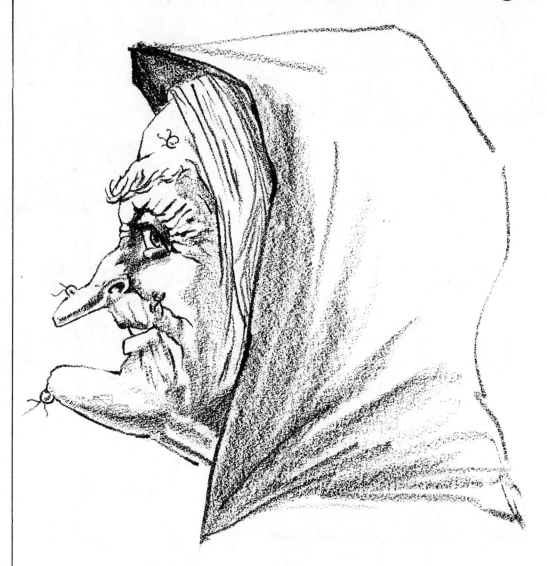

Chapter 35

Materials:
- Castor oil
- Green oil clay, medium grade
- Modeling tools
- Textured sponge
- Alcohol
- Fine sandpaper

Construction:

1. After the plaster mold has dried for twenty-four hours, coat it with castor oil and let it stand for ten minutes; wipe off most of the oil, leaving just a thin film. This helps the clay adhere to the plaster.

Prosthetics

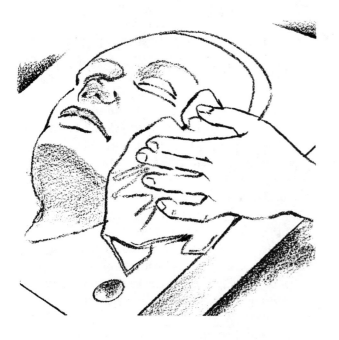

2. To begin modeling: Every professional makeup artist has a morgue or picture file to refer to for ideas and suggestions. Choose the pictures that best portray the character you wish to create and display pictures for study.

3. Add little pieces of clay to the plaster head until you have roughed in the approximate size and shape of the prosthetic desired.

5. While modeling, it's essential never to make an undercut. An undercut is an area where the top and bottom plaster molds will lock together. Be positive that the top mold will pull directly off; you do this by frequently viewing the modeling from immediately overhead and testing the depth by inserting a pin through the clay. The areas to be extremely careful with are found around the nostrils, inside the nose, under the chin, and in back of the jaws.

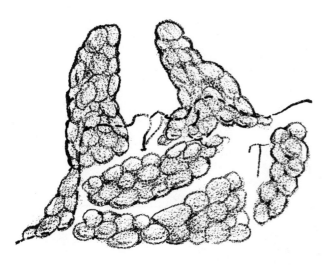

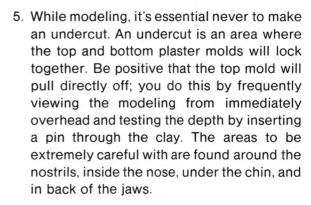

4. With the modeling tools, start to develop the finished model, and smooth it out with fine sandpaper as you progress. Constantly refer to the pictures for detail. Your own ability to perceive line, form, and shape is extremely important in creating the prosthetic.

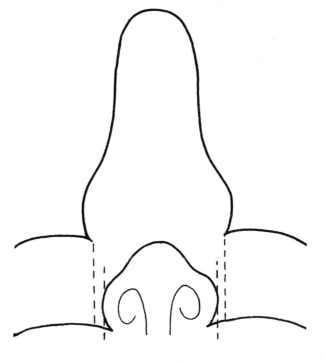

Modeling with Clay

6. To smooth out the modeling, use alcohol on the ends of the fingers and rub out all the rough spots.

7. For a final touch, the modeling should be stippled for texture. Textured sponges are made by taking rubber impressions of objects that have texture; fruit is commonly used. Tie a string around the head of a nail and push it into a rough-skinned orange or grapefruit. Dip the fruit into liquid latex, remove, let dry, and dip again. Five or six dippings should be sufficient. When the final coat of latex dries, powder it, cut it, and remove the fruit; then turn the latex shell inside out. The inside will have acquired an impression of natural skin texture; press this texture into the clay modeling with your fingers. I cannot overemphasize the need for careful observation, creative sculpturing patience, and a painstaking workmanship in modeling with clay. All of the imperfections left in the modeling will unfortunately appear in the completed prosthetic.

Prosthetics.

Casting the Negative Mold

Chapter 36

CASING THE MOLD

Materials:
  Wet clay
  Modeling tools
  Cotton swabs
  Alcohol

Application:

1. The term "casing" means applying a thin coat of wet clay, approximately ¼ inch thick, over most of the exposed plaster. This does not include the sides of the mold.

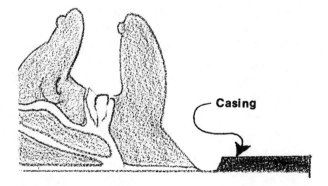

Casing

2. Between the character modeling made of oil clay and the wet clay, ¼ inch of plaster should be exposed. Also, at least 4 square inches of plaster should be exposed on

each corner where the round keys were carved.

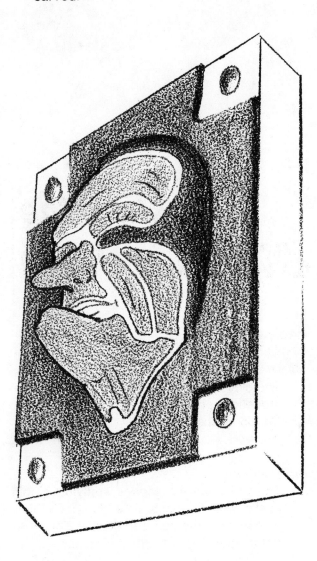

Clear acrylic spray
Prepared Vaseline petroleum jelly

Application:
1. Over all the exposed plaster, including the sides, paint a coat of thinned lacquer and allow lacquer to dry.

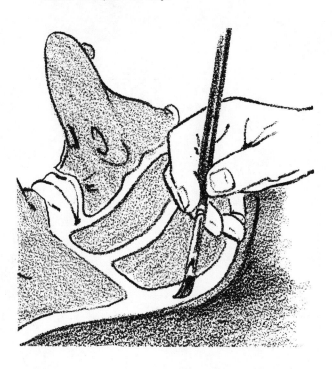

2. Spray a light film of clear acrylic over all the clay and allow acrylic to dry.

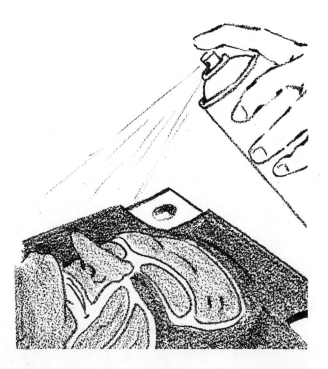

3. All exposed plaster should be cleaned with cotton swabs dipped in alcohol.
4. The purpose of casing is to relieve the surface tension created when the prosthetic is made; the casing will allow the molds to separate easily. The ¼ inch of exposed plaster surrounding the character modeling is used as a cutoff line when you pour the foaming materials; the exposed plaster corners are used for support.

PREPARING THE CASED MOLD

Materials:
Lacquer and thinner 50/50
Small brush

Prosthetics

3. Over the exposed lacquered plaster, paint a thin coat of prepared Vaseline.
   NOTE: It is important that the exposed plaster be sealed and greased, or else the new wet plaster to be applied will bond to itself, making it impossible to separate the molds.
   REMEMBER: Do not get prepared Vaseline on the oil clay.

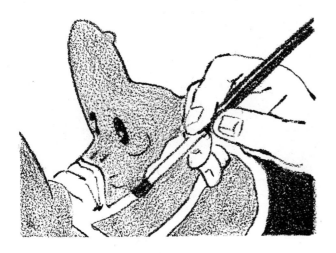

CASTING THE NEGATIVE MOLD

Materials:

Hydrocal Plaster (a hard-setting plaster) or dental stone
Plastic bowl, 5 by 12½ inches
3 quarts water
Kitchen knife, blunt edge
1-inch brush

Construction:

1. Mix the plaster as explained in Chapter 33.
2. Brush the first coat of plaster over the top of the clay and greased plaster. Wash out the brush. Continue to add plaster as it starts to set. The entire negative plaster mold should be at least 1½ inches thick, especially on the corners.

   NOTE: If the mold is to be used for foam rubber, the first coat should be about ½ inch thick; allow the first layer to partially harden, then apply a 1-inch coat of plaster and fiber over the other.

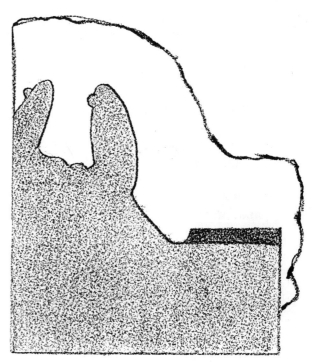

3. With the kitchen knife, smooth out the surface and square the sides so that they are even with the bottom half; there should be absolutely no overhang. Work quickly with the plaster, or it will harden unfinished and in an undesirable form.

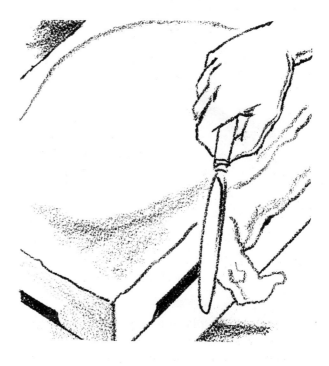

4. Allow the mold to cool or to dry overnight before opening it.

OPENING THE MOLD AND CLEANING

Materials:
- Kitchen oven (warm heat)
- Hammer
- Chisel or wood wedge
- Alcohol
- Stiff bristle brush, rags, cotton swabs
- Wood modeling tools

Construction:

1. Preheat the oven to "warm," insert the mold, and allow it to remain until it has warmed all the way through. This takes about twenty to thirty minutes. The purpose of the warming is to soften the oil clay to expedite separation.
2. Place the mold on a flat surface and gently tap between the halves with a chisel or wedge, forcing the two sides apart.

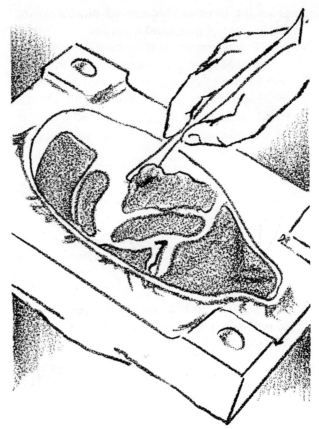

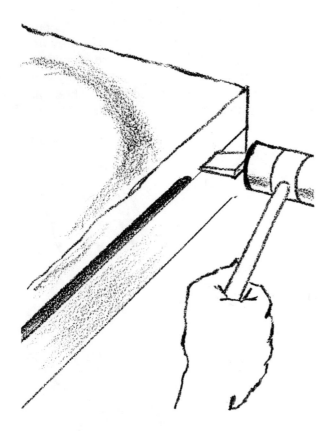

5. With the brush, rags, and alcohol, remove all residual clay.

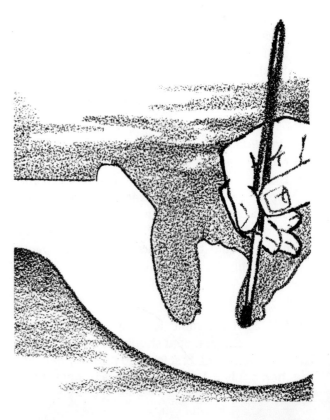

3. Carefully lift off the negative top section and turn it over.
4. With the wood modeling tools, remove all the clay. Save the green clay for future projects, and discard any dry clay.

Prosthetics

6. Put the two halves back together until you are ready to form the prosthetic.

7. Chipped or broken plaster edges can be glued into place with an adhesive called "Plaster Weld."

Construction of a Prosthetic

Chapter 37

A recent speedy procedure for constructing theatrical prosthetics involves liquid latex and flexible polyurethane. Both foam rubber and polyurethane have their advantages and disadvantages. After studying the two styles of prosthetics, choose the one that best satisfies the budget, available time, and specific need.

Polyfoam must be stored and mixed at approximately 60 to 80°F. If the polyfoam is too cold, it will retard the setting; conversely, if it is too hot, the reaction will occur rapidly. Avoid breathing the vapors of polyfoam; use only in a well-ventilated room.

POLYURETHANE- PROSTHETICS

Materials:
    Liquid latex
    Polyurethane (polyfoam)
    Small disposable brush
    Silicone grease

Color (compatibie coloring tints)
Portable hair dryer
Small paper cups and stirring stick
Rubber glue (adhesive)
Measuring jars (baby food jars showing measurements)
Measuring spoons
Newspapers

Construction:
1. Generously spread out the newspapers. Polyurethane is highly adhesive, and everything near it should be protected.
2. Add one drop of color to 5 ounces of latex and stir thoroughly.
3. Brush one thin coat of colored latex over both the inside negative and positive molds, making sure that all the plaster is covered except for the corners. (*Caution:* Do not paint any latex over the keys or corners of either side.)

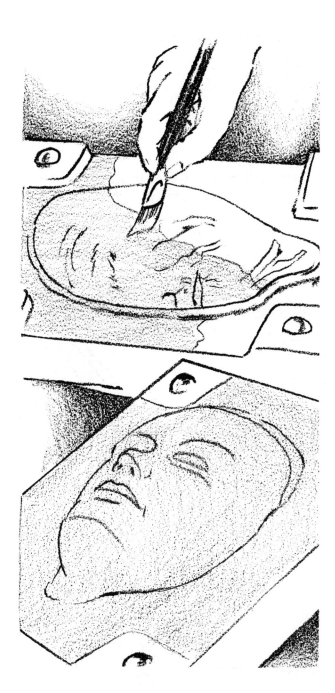

7. Where the edge around the prosthetic will form, paint a thin coat of adhesive on both sides and allow to semidry.

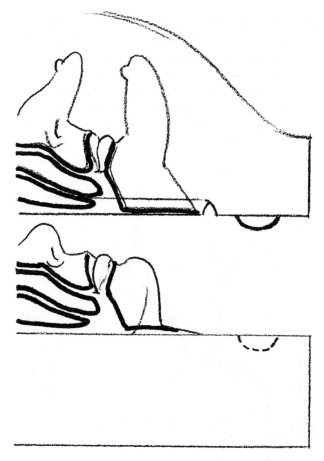

4. Dry latex with the hair dryer.
5. Paint a second coat of latex, touching up any white spots missed the first time. Allow to dry. When preparing a mold with a latex skin for polyfoam keep the dried latex absolutely clean, because powder and grease will prevent the polyfoam from adhering.
6. With your finger, thinly coat the keys or corners on both molds with silicone grease. The two coats of latex and the grease act as a release agent for the polyfoam, which readily adheres to plaster.

8. For small prosthetics, such as a facial mask, mix one ounce of polyfoam to one-fourth

teaspoon of a setting agent in a paper cup and stir until it becomes cloudy, approximately five to ten seconds. Quickly pour the mixed liquid into the negative side of the mold.

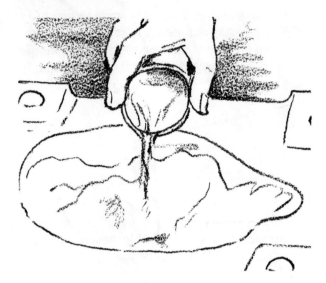

9. Fit the positive mold into place and secure by hand or with loose clamps. The molds should be held firmly until the foaming action ceases, about ten minutes; then the molds should be carefully set aside for one hour. During the first ten minutes any jarring or other movement will cause the polyfoam to collapse.

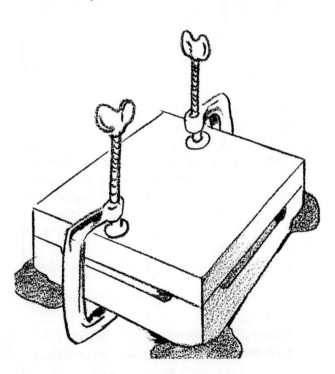

Separating the Polyfoam Mold

Materials:
   Chisel or wood wedges
   Hammer
   Scissors

Procedure:
   1. After one hour you can separate the molds by carefully prying the edges apart.

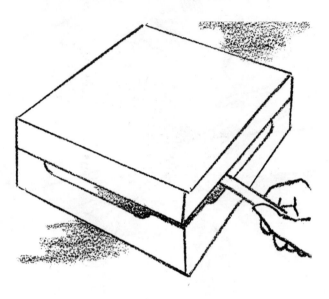

2. Remove the prosthetic carefully so that the latex skin won't separate from the polyfoam.

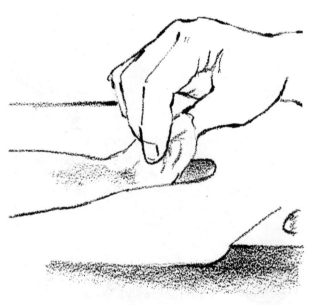

3. With the scissors cut excess latex and polyfoam away from the edges of the prosthetic.

Prosthetics

To create a thinner edge after trimming away the excess, separate the two latex skins and trim away the edge of the inside one.

4. If there is a separation of latex skin from the polyurethane, apply latex adhesive between the two layers and press together.

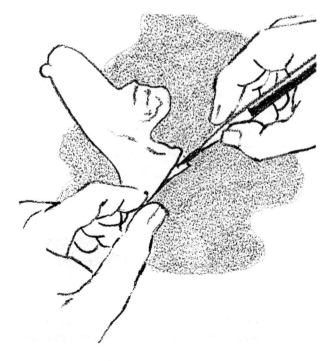

Cleaning up the Mold

Material:
Acetone

Method:
1. Remove any excess latex from the mold.
2. Remove any escaped polyfoam that has become attached to the plaster mold; it should be removed with a cotton swab saturated in acetone.

FOAM LATEX

Another process for constructing prosthetics, which is more costly and time consuming, is a special latex called "foam latex." It has an advantage over the polyfoam process in that the edges can be made finer and the finished piece is softer. The basic formulas and mixing procedures vary from manufacturer to manufacturer. Specific instructions for use should be included with each purchase.

The following process applies to most foam latex formulas.

Materials:
Castor oil and brush
Cheesecloth

Talc
Cotton swabs
Liquid latex
Liquid foam latex and additives
Electric mixer and bowl
Latex color
Measuring equipment: scales, weights, and
    glassware
Circulating or kitchen oven

Preparation of mold:
1. After constructing and drying the negative
   and positive sections of the mold, coat them
   both with castor oil. Remove excess oil by
   wiping clean.
2. Powder both sides with a fine talc or baby
   powder. Blow off the excess.
3. With a cotton swab and liquid latex, paint
   only the negative plaster surface on the
   prosthetic. Pour liquid into deep molds.
   Drain and clean off any spilled excess.

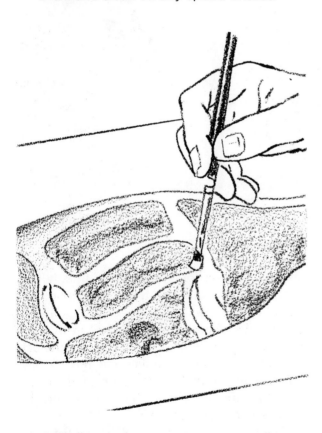

4. Allow the mold to stand and begin to pre-
   pare the foam latex.

Mixing Foam Latex
1. The process consists of mixing several

chemicals with the liquid foam latex in a
clean mixing bowl. Cleanliness is important,
because even the smallest particle left over
can spoil the complete process.
2. Place the bowl in the electric mixer on high
   speed, and beat until the latex has developed into a high foam, approximately ten
   minutes. Be sure to protect all clothing and
   surrounding surfaces, since latex is difficult
   to remove from porous materials.
3. Measure all chemicals accurately into separate containers.
4. Once the latex has been highly whipped,
   turn the mixer speed down very slowly to
   gradually remove any air bubbles (approximately five minutes).
5. Pour the material into the negative side of
   the mold, set the positive side in place, and
   secure.

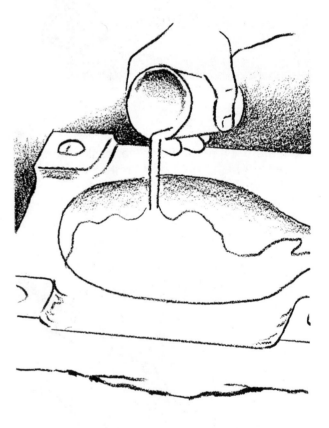

6. Allow the mold to rest until the latex has
   stiffened.
7. Curing: Hot curing of foam latex is essential.
   A circulating oven with a temperature of
   200°F should be used; if a regular oven is
   used, set thermostat at 200°F, place a pan
   of water inside the oven, and leave the door

slightly ajar to release the steam. Continue to add water as it evaporates. Steam curing or circulating heat are the best methods for setting the latex; other techniques may ruin the mold.

10. Remove the prosthetic, squeeze it by hand, and allow it to stand until all the moisture has evaporated. After squeezing, if the latex prosthetic does not return to its original shape, it was not baked long enough.

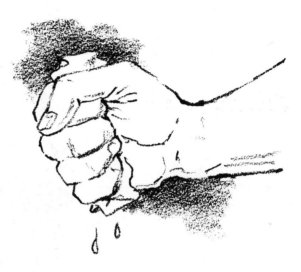

8. Small molds (e.g., nose) will cure in the oven within two hours; larger ones (e.g., full face) require an extra hour or more.

9. Removal: After baking, remove the mold with protective pads or gloves; gently pry open.

11. Coat both sides of the hot mold with castor oil to replace plaster moisture removed by the heat.

12. When the piece has dried, it is ready for application.

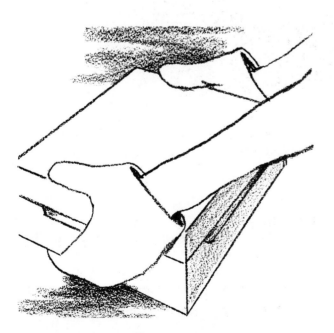

Application of a Prosthetic

It is essential that the specific steps for applying the completed prosthetic be followed in sequence.

Materials:
- Liquid latex
- Red lining pencil
- Grease makeup
- Modeling wax
- Powder and puff
- Latex sponge, cut into 2-inch triangles
- Spirit gum, with large and small brush
- Hand dryer
- Cotton

Application:
1. Apply a thin coat of base makeup to the face (grease).
2. Fit the prosthetic to the face; mark a red line with the pencil around all edges and openings.

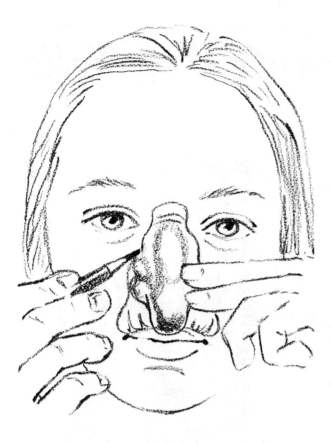

5. Paint a coat of spirit gum over the dry latex on the face, and fit the prosthetic to the face. *Do not* paint where the edges will lie, because if they become stuck, it is difficult to release them.

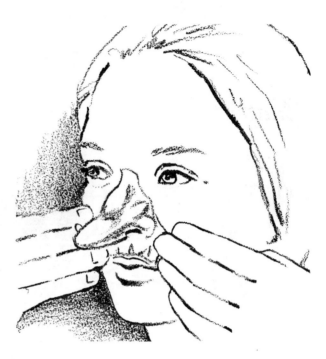

3. If applying a prosthetic over the eyebrows, work wax into eyebrows to cover and protect them.
4. Within the red lines, stipple a thin coat of latex on the face with the triangular sponge; dry the latex, and powder.

Fit the piece to the face, and with a small brush apply spirit gum underneath; then gently press the edges down and into place with a damp powder puff. A pair of tweezers will also help to straighten rolled edges.

For larger pieces, paint and adhere spirit gum in sections, starting with the nose, under and around the eyes, forehead, sides of face, mouth, and chin.

7. Thoroughly dry and powder.

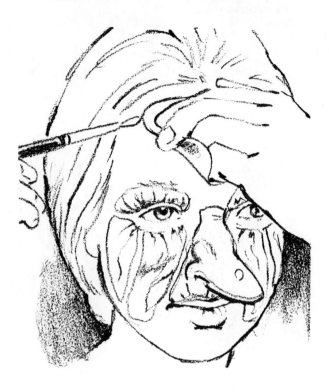

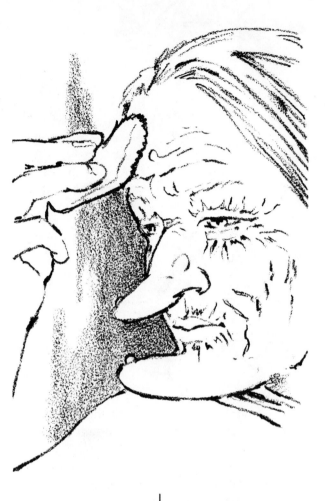

6. Around and over all of the edges of the prosthetic, stipple a thin coat of latex; you may need to make several applications to achieve an even blend with the face. To make the blend even, if an edge is too high, fill the gap with wax or rubberized cotton before stippling.

Makeup for the Prosthetic

Chapter 39

Materials:

Plastic sealer or surgical spray bandage

Hand dryer

Powder and puff

Rubber mask grease (commercial or self-mixed)

Assorted brushes

White latex sponge

Stipple sponge

Various cosmetics needed to complete the character to be portrayed

Method:

1. For security, paint all rubber with a coat of plastic sealer or surgical spray dressing; then apply the rubber mask grease.

   Rubber mask grease can be used without sealing, but there is a possibility of the prosthetic turning light. Heavy makeup such as this should be smoothed and blended with a stipple-like action.

3. Powder heavily with translucent powder to absorb all the oil in the makeup. Brush off the excess; remove any traces by lightly patting the surface with a damp sponge.
4. Continue to make up the prosthetic and face as you would a straight base or character makeup; add stippled colors to it to achieve natural skin tone and texture.

2. Apply highlights and shadows for contrast and contour. Blend them thoroughly with the base makeup.

5. Large prosthetics can be made up and then applied. Do not allow makeup to get on or around the edges to be glued down. After application merely make up the edges and the exposed skin.
6. For added realism, prepunch hair into the prosthetic before applying it. Use the same technique given for the hair-punched bald cap, Chapter 29.

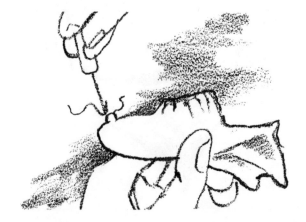

Prosthetics

7. It is impossible to get hair and hair lace to adhere to a prosthetic if there is any grease makeup on it, because grease acts as a separator. When painting adhesive on a prosthetic, do it on a clean area, or powder the makeup heavily to absorb any oil. Do not overwork adhesive that has been painted on a prosthetic; allow it to partially dry so the hair or lace will adhere to it.

SECTION FIVE REVIEW

1. Name four types of materials used to construct facial prosthetics; list their individual characteristics.
2. Define two types of facial impression materials, and describe their specific properties.
3. Collect twelve pictures for your file exemplifying nationalities, historical beards and moustaches, and unusual characters.
4. With reference to facial casting, evaluate the following statements:

    a. A coat of Vaseline petroleum jelly must be applied over the entire face before the face is cast.   T   F

    b. One material used for supporting impression material is plaster bandage   T   F

    c. To properly mix plaster, stir each handful with water as the plaster is sifted into the bowl.   T   F

    d. The same moulage may be thinned with water and reused many times.   T   F

    e. It is always necessary to seal the cast when applying wet plaster over already-hardened plaster.   T   F

    f. For strength, the negative plaster mold should be at least $1\frac{1}{2}$ inches thick.   T   F

    g. The best tools for cleaning a plaster life mask are made of metal.   T   F

    h. Tools must be cleaned immediately when you work with wet plaster.   T   F

5. What does prepared Vaseline petroleum jelly consist of, and what is the ratio of these ingredients?
6. Define and diagram an undercut.
7. Concerning the construction of a prosthetic, judge the following sentences:

    a. The best releases for polyfoam are silicone grease and latex.   T   F

    b. When painting latex on the molds, both sides should be completely covered, including the corners.   T   F

    c. The best implement for mixing foam rubber is a wire whisk.   T   F

    d. After the final chemical has been mixed into polyfoam or foam latex, the material must be poured immediately.   T   F

8. From the beginning of the curing cycle, how soon can a polyfoam or a foam latex prosthetic be applied?
9. What are the advantages and disadvantages of polyfoam versus foam latex?
10. With reference to making up a prosthetic:

    a. What is the best makeup to cover a latex prosthetic with?

    b. Is makeup for prosthetics very oily?

    c. What material is used as a protective sealant before the makeup is applied?

    d. Describe the motion used to apply makeup for the best coverage on a prosthetic.

Conclusion

Theatrical makeup is an illusionary art. Like other arts, it can be perfected only through training, study, and practice. As a performer, you owe it to yourself to gain proficiency in every area that will help you to create a role: voice training and interpretation, body control, costume, etc. Theatrical makeup contributes a marvelous and unique boost to your performance. It makes both you and the audience already believe that you are the character. Cultivate this gratifying art; and never attempt anything less than perfection.

Supply Sources

THEATRICAL SUPPLIERS FOR COSMETICS, WIGS, HAIRGOODS, AND LATEX

1. Paramount Theatrical Supplies
   Alcone Company, Inc.
   32 West 20th Street
   New York, New York 10011
2. Olesen Company
   1535 Ivar Avenue
   Hollywood, California 90028

BEAUTY SUPPLIERS FOR COSMETICS AND HAIRGOODS

1. Jack Spirling Beauty Supply
   13639 Vanowen
   Van Nuys, California 91405
   Distributor of Clens, Nextel simulated blood, and Bob Kelly Cosmetics
2. Frends Beauty Supply
   5202 Laurel Canyon Blvd.
   North Hollywood, California 91607
   Distributor of Clens, Nextel simulated blood

COSMETICS

1. Max Factor
   1655 North McCadden Place
   Hollywood, California 90028

2. Bob Kelly Cosmetic Co.
   151 West 46th Street
   New York, New York 10036
   Distributor of wigs, hairgoods and makeup kits
3. Ben Nye Studio
   11571 Santa Monica Blvd.
   West Los Angeles, California 90025
   Distributor of makeup kits

WIGS

1. Favian Hair Inc.
   6542 Greenbrush Avenue
   Van Nuys, California 91401
   Rentals
2. Ira Senz Wigs
   580 5th Avenue
   New York, New York 10036

PROSTHETIC MATERIALS

1. Douglas & Sturgess
   730 Bryant Street
   San Francisco, California 94107
   Distributor of moulage and related materials
2. Johnson & Johnson
   New Brunswick, New Jersey
   Distributor of plaster bandage and clear tape
3. Don Post Studio
   10940½ Burbank Blvd.
   North Hollywood, California 91601

Distributor of latex, polyfoam, masks, and latex bald caps

4. Scientific Surgical Supply
15137 Califa Street
Van Nuys, California 91401
Distributor of plaster bandage, clear tape, plastic spray bandage

5. S.S. White Dental Supply
A Division of Pennwalt Corp.
1138 Wilshire Blvd.
Los Angeles, California 90017
Distributor of duplicating compound, alginate, and dental stone (plaster)

ARTIST SUPPLIES

Carter Sexton, Inc.
5308 Laural Canyon Blvd.
North Hollywood, California 91607

MAKEUP SPECIALTIES

John Chambers Studio
330 South Myers Street
Burbank, California 91506
Distributor of plastic bald caps, plastic scar material, and custom masks

INDEX

74
75
76

89

89